AD HOC NETWORKS

Edited by **Jesús Hamilton Ortiz**
and **Álvaro Pachón de la Cruz**

Ad Hoc Networks
http://dx.doi.org/10.5772/62746
Edited by Jesús Hamilton Ortiz and Álvaro Pachón de la Cruz

Contributors

Subhrananda Goswami, Chandan Bikash Das, Subhankar Joardar, Dibyendu Kumar Pal, Samarjit Kar, Chao Gao, Guorong Zhao, Jianhua Lu, Rutvij H. Jhaveri, Narendra M. Patel, Devesh C. Jinwala, Rasa Bruzgiene, Lina Narbutaite, Tomas Adomkus, Christian Poellabauer, Mehdi Golestanian, Joshua Siva, Kun Xie, Xin Wang, Shiming He, Keqin Li, Dafang Zhang

Published by InTech
Janeza Trdine 9, 51000 Rijeka, Croatia

Publishing Process Manager Diana Olloni
Technical Editor SPi Global
Cover InTech Design team

First published April, 2017
Printed in Croatia
Legal deposit, Croatia: National and University Library in Zagreb

Additional hard copies can be obtained from orders@intechopen.com

Ad Hoc Networks, Edited by Jesús Hamilton Ortiz and Álvaro Pachón de la Cruz
p. cm.
Print ISBN 978-953-51-3109-0
Online ISBN 978-953-51-3110-6

For EU product safety concerns:
IN TECH d.o.o., Prolaz Marije Krucifikse Kozulić 3, 51000 Rijeka, Croatia,
info@intechopen.com or visit our website at intechopen.com.

Meet the editors

Jesús Hamilton Ortiz earned his Bachelor's degree in Mathematics and Electrical Engineering from the Universidades Santiago de Cali and Universidad del Valle in Cali Colombia. He then went on to earn a D.E. in Telematics Engineering from the Universidad Politécnica de Madrid, and a Ph.D. in Computer Engineering from the Universidad de Castilla la Mancha. In 2016 he earned his Ph.D in Telecommunication Engineering from the Universidad Autonoma de Madrid. He is working in a Ph.D and Post-doc position at the Universidad Politecnica de Cataluña. Dr. Ortiz is a reviewer, Editorial Board member and has published research in several international journals. He has edited four books and is working on a fifth one currently. He is the founder of Closemobile R&D. S.M.E. which focuses on telecommunication and aerospace science. With Closemobile he is developing several projects on UAV's, VANET and Wireless Networks.

Álvaro Pachón is a professor at the ICESI University, Colombia. He received his B.S. degree in Computer Engineering from ICESI University in 1990. He went on to receive his D.E.A. and Ph.D.
in Information Technologies from Vigo University, Spain in 2005 and 2015, respectfully.

Contents

Preface

An Ad Hoc network is an autonomous system made up by a set of nodes (mobile or fixed) which use wireless bonds to communicate. These nodes constitute a temporal network without the necessity of a centralized administration, nor the standard group of regular services usually offered by the conventional networks (address assignment, safety, name services, etc). In the case of MANETs (Mobile Ad Hoc networks), the network nodes can move on an aleatory way to organize itself arbitrarily. Therefore, the network's topology can change in an incredibly fast, dynamic and unpredictable way.

Ad Hoc wireless network properties must be taken into account when considering proposals for service improvement and protocol designs. Some of these properties include: node mobile capacity, which promotes dynamic topology (referring to the MANETs), the routing network's demeanor, which shows multiple hops, a broadband's limited restrictions, operational power restrictions, limited physical security, and limited scalability. Some advantages of Ad Hoc wireless networks include: quick deployment, dynamic topology, a high failure tolerance, an easy way for connectivity, mobility, deployment costs, and a chance to re-use the spectrum. Some issues related to the use of Ad Hoc wireless networks are: broadband restrictions, processing capability, power restrictions, a high-rate of latency, transmission errors, a lack of security, location and roaming (only occurs with MANETs).

Ad Hoc wireless networks are useful in multiple situations including: at conferences and meetings where people use laptops, at home with the use of smart household appliances, in search and rescue operations, in cases of natural disasters, or on a battlefield. In these situations, the benefits of the system can truly be utilized due to the system's versatility and ability of quick deployment.

A systematic review of Ad Hoc wireless networks allows for the consideration of the following issues:

a) Operative Characteristics: This type of network does not rely on an infrastructure, instead, it has a broadcast information channel, with some restrictions in the use of resources (storage power and broadband) which derive from its precariousness. With MANETs, node dynamics display a variable topology, there is no central place to connect or coordinate the allocation and the use of resources. This fact promotes the establishment of distributed schemes for the assignment and use of resources, favoring the spontaneous appearance of a global coordination mechanism, called self-organization, resulting from 1 ocal interactions between the initially disordered components. This type of distributed organization is very robust and allows them to survive and self-repair in the event of operational damage or disruption.

b) Its modeling: The complex operation of this type of network, derived from the permanent change in the channel and its topology, requires the development of models that allow characterization of its behavior. Four major types of models must be developed: the behavior model of the channel, which tries to predict the behavior of the signal propagating; the mobility model of the nodes, which establishes the way each node moves in the geographical area where the MANET is deployed; the traffic pattern generation model, which describes how information is generated at each of the nodes; and the model of energy consumption, which establishes the effect of the mobility of the nodes and the traffic patterns on the energy consumption of the battery.

c) Network's routing type: The characteristics described for a network's routing type are particularly complex in this type of network. Two types of approaches have been proposed, the proactive and reactive approach. A proactive approach establishes and updates routes in tables before the need to deliver information to a destination arises. The changing nature of the network topology causes, in many cases, a loss in the effort to maintain the trajectories. The reactive approach establishes and updates the routes in the tables only at the moment in which the need to take information to a destination arises. In this case, a little delay is generated as a consequence of the need to determine the path to the destination when the need arises. Some other important criteria are also taken into account when proposing a routing protocol, including: resilience, overload, security, performance, delay, resource utilization and, ultimately, energy consumption. Also, proposals are developed considering other key characteristics in the routing: the mobility of the nodes (network dynamics), the quality of service in the routing, security, the consideration of the state of the channel and energy consumption. Also, dynamic addressing schemes need to be considered when using both the IPv4 protocol and the IPv6 protocol.

d) Evaluation of benefits: Development of metrics that allow the evaluation of the following metrics: throughput, end-to-end delay, packet delivery rate, network load level and packet loss rate. These metrics are affected by the type of routing, the behavior of the nodes (their dynamics and their speed), the size of the network, and the number of traffic sources, among other factors.

e) The key aspects associated with operation are related to: offering quality service to deployed applications, the allocation schemes of resources within this type of network, power management, seeking energy efficiency, and security in the exchange of information. In terms of quality of service, this type of network offers significant challenges that require the development of models, protocols and metrics that allow the evaluation and guarantee of the service levels expected by the applications and services that are deployed in this type of network. In terms of resource allocation schemes, it is important to note that the variable behavior of these networks requires dynamic mechanisms for the allocation of resources. In particular, dynamic spectrum allocation and resource allocation schemes considering channel behavior.

In terms of security, it is necessary to develop architectures and models that guarantee the safe provision of services in these types of networks. To get this, the risks must being identified to establish the strategies that allow mitigating them and surviving the different types of attacks.

f) Simulation tools and test scenarios: The complex nature of the behavior of this type of network forces the development of behavioral models and test scenarios to validate hypotheses and to show how the nodes and the network will behave.

In conclusion, the universe of Ad Hoc networks is complex, full of great challenges and problems to be solved. This book presents a perspective of different applications, in different areas of knowledge.

Jesús Hamilton Ortiz, PhD
Santiago de Cali University
Columbia

Álvaro Pachón de la Cruz, PhD
ICESI University
Columbia

Section 1

Protocols

Chapter 1

Data-Gathering and Aggregation Protocol for Networked Carrier Ad Hoc Networks: The Optimal and Heuristic Approach

Chao Gao, Guorong Zhao and Jianhua Lu

Additional information is available at the end of the chapter

http://dx.doi.org/10.5772/66641

Abstract

In this chapter, we address the problem of data-gathering and aggregation (DGA) in navigation carrier ad hoc networks (NC-NET), in order to reduce energy consumption and enhance network scalability and lifetime. Several clustering algorithms have been presented for vehicle ad hoc network (VANET) and other mobile ad hoc network (MANET). However, DGA approach in harsh environments, in terms of long-range transmission, high dynamic topology and three-dimensional monitor region, is still an open issue. In this chapter, we propose a novel clustering-based DGA approach, namely, distributed multiple-weight data-gathering and aggregation (DMDG) protocol, to guarantee quality of service (QoS)-aware DGA for heterogeneous services in above harsh environments. Our approach is explored by the synthesis of three kernel features. First, the network model is addressed according to specific conditions of networked carrier ad hoc networks (NC-NET), and several performance indicators are selected. Second, a distributed multiple-weight data-gathering and aggregation protocol (DMDG) is proposed, which contains all-sided active clustering scheme and realizes long-range real-time communication by tactical data link under a time-division multiple access/carrier sense multiple access (TDMA/CSMA) channel sharing mechanism. Third, an analytical paradigm facilitating the most appropriate choice of the next relay is proposed. Experimental results have shown that DMDG scheme can balance the energy consumption and extend the network lifetime notably and outperform LEACH, PEACH and DEEC in terms of network lifetime and coverage rate, especially in sparse node density or anisotropic topologies.

Keywords: navigation carrier ad hoc networks (NC-NET), clustering protocol, data-gathering and aggregation (DGA), QoS aware

1. Introduction

The emerging advantages of wireless network inspire other technical fields to solve their own bottlenecks through the network approach [1]. In our researches, we devote to put forward a network-aware solution for a bottleneck of modern navigation technology, which restricts it from stage of a higher level [2]. That is, the level of navigation efficiency is closely related to self-contained degree of navigation system; on one hand, the upgrade of its integrity will increase the burdens on economic investment and physical load; on the other hand, if we simplify the complexity of navigation equipment to alleviate the above burdens, its navigation capacity will be degraded accordingly. In previous works [2–6], we have proposed a novel network architecture, namely, navigation carrier ad hoc networks (NC-NET), to handle the navigation-related issues, in terms of cooperative navigation, localization, target tracking and multimedia data exchange, through a network approach. The proposed NC-NET, which is essentially ad hoc network between navigation carriers (NCs), is surveyed as a new network family. Hereinto, navigation carrier is defined as the carrier that has the demands of localization and/or navigation, such as aircraft, car, ship, submarine, buoyage system, satellite or pseudo satellite, etc. In Refs. [2, 3], we have finished partial protocols and mechanisms as follows: (i) the protocol framework and the models in physical layer [2]; (ii) a diffserv-based dynamic cooperative MAC protocol, i.e., DDC-MAC [3]; and (iii) the network-based localization mechanisms [4–6]. As part of a series of research work, the main objective of this chapter is to develop a data-gathering and aggregation (DGA) protocol with full account of the unique challenges in NC-NET.

In previous literature, the DGA problem has been investigated extensively [7–12], to prioritize and manage the resource sharing according to the unique requirements of each traffic class. However, in DGA of NC-NET, we should integrate into account several unique challenges that never handled in existing work, including (i) coexistence of multiple traffic services with heterogeneous QoS requests; (ii) coexistence of short-range and long-range traffic requests; and (iii) harsh routing environment, i.e., sparse network density, long-range transmission and high dynamic topology.

Several clustering algorithms are presented for VANET such as [13–26]. However, these algorithms do not show how the routing is performed according to their clustering algorithms after the cluster formation. Hence, they do not guarantee the network topology during the routing process. Their clustering algorithms ignore as well the quality of service requirements important for safety, emergency and multimedia services. On the other hand, QoS-based clustering algorithms take into consideration the quality of service metrics such as bandwidth, energy and end-to-end delay to group the nodes. However, they ignore the high speed mobility metrics which makes them inefficient to deal with NC-NET. The optimized link state routing (OLSR) [15] is a proactive routing protocol that has been modeled to cope with mobile ad hoc networks (MANETs). Its basic idea is to elect a cluster head for each group of neighbour nodes and divide hence the network into clusters. These heads then select a set of specialized nodes called multipoint relays (MPRs). The function of the MPR nodes is to reduce the overhead of flooding messages by minimizing the duplicate transmissions within the same zone. QoS-OLSR [17] is an enhanced version of OLSR that extends the MANET network lifetime taking into consideration the available bandwidth and the residual energy per node during cluster head election and MPR node selection. Nonetheless, this protocol does not consider the mobility of nodes while computing the QoS. Thus, nodes with high bandwidth, energy and mobility may be elected as cluster heads which leads to recurrent disconnections. Likewise, the MPRs selected according to this protocol do not satisfy both mobility constraints and routing parameters (end-to-end delay and packet delivery ratio). Moreover, the MPR selection algorithm according to QoS-OLSR is vulnerable to cheating in the sense that some nodes may claim bogus QoS values in order to ensure being selected as MPRs. Furthermore, QoS-OLSR does not advance any MPR recovery algorithm able to select quick alternatives and keep the network connected in case of link failures.

With these comparisons, it is clear that the results on challenge (i), challenge (ii) and their hybrid are extensive; however, in harsh environment that of challenge (iii), the integrated investigates on challenges (i) and (ii) are quite limited. From above analysis, we identify the missing properties in the existing work for QoS provisioning in NC-NET and introduce the design and implementation of a new distributed multiple-weight data-gathering and aggregation protocol (DMDG) protocol for NC-NET. DMDG is designed with key features to support the above three challenges. These features include the following: first, the network model is addressed according to specific conditions of networked carrier ad hoc networks (NC-NET), and several performance indicators are selected. Second, a distributed multiple-weight data-gathering and aggregation protocol (DMDG) is proposed, which contains all-sided active clustering scheme and realizes long-range real-time communication by tactical data link under a TDMA/CSMA channel sharing mechanism. Third, an analytical paradigm facilitating the most appropriate choice of the next relay is proposed. To optimize the performance of DMDG, the aforementioned contributions are theoretically analysed and evaluated. Finally, the results demonstrate the efficiency of our protocol by comparing to other contemporary MANET routing protocols. Experimental results have shown that DMDG scheme can balance the energy consumption and extend the network lifetime notably and outperform LEACH, PEACH and DEEC in terms of network lifetime and coverage rate, especially in sparse node density or anisotropic topologies.

The remainder of this chapter is organized as follows. Section 2 introduces the network model and evaluates indicators of NC-NET. Section 3 presents the details of the proposed DMDG protocol, including the clustering algorithm, data aggregation and communication scheme and the three-dimensional routing algorithm. Section 4 presents the numerical analysis and simulation of our scheme, along with the corresponding results. Finally, in Section 5, we summarize this chapter with conclusions and prospect.

2. Network model and problem formulations

In the area of cluster-based wireless sensor networks, the previous research is quite extensive, with energy efficiency and scalability being the main focus of many of the clustering protocols proposed so far [6–10]. Meanwhile, much research has been done on sensor activation protocols, which focus on selecting a subset of the active sensor nodes that are sufficient to satisfy the network's coverage requirements. Compare to traditional ad hoc network, NC-NET has special characters in a couple of aspects, including high-powered links, high-speed nodes and sparse and very-large-scale working range. In this section, we discuss the related work that has been done taking into account these points.

2.1. Network model

In this subsection, we first introduce the characteristics of ad hoc network and then define the network model of navigation carrier ad hoc network. We model the ad hoc network as a graph, $G = (C, E, R_c)$, which consists of a set of mobile nodes, $C = \{C_1, C_2, \cdots, C_m\}$, and a set of wireless links, E; each sensor node consists of components of sensing, computing and wireless transmission. Assume that each node has the same transmission radius R_t and the same sensing radius R_s. The notations used in this chapter are defined in **Table 1**.

Before discussing the nature of this problem, we give the following assumptions for the feasibility of the NC-NET, which include monitor area, transmission channel and communication environment.

Assumption 1 (Monitor area). The monitor area of NC-NET A_c is a cylinder, which is equivalent with the tradition definition of monitoring area.

$$A_c = \{(x, y, z)|x^2 + y^2 \leq R_{\text{cov}}, 0 \leq z \leq h_{\text{cov}}\} \tag{1}$$

where R_{cov} is monitor radius and h_{cov} is monitor height.

Assumption 2 (Signal link). The transmission path adopts tactical data link. To meet the requirement of real-time performance and reliability, R_c is defined as 1/3 – 1/5 ratio to the effective transmission radius of the link and assumed that the bit error rate (BER) is invariable.

Assumption 3 (Communication environment). The statistical property of the NLOS propagation accords with exponential distribution, while the time delay accords with Bernoulli distribution. The coupling and interference in electromagnetic environment are mutually independent white noise with zero mean.

Figure 1 is an example of NC-NET, in which the type of area coverage A_{c-1} is considered. $A_{c-1} \subset A_c$ and d_{ch-ch}, d_{ch-M}, d_{ch-unk}, d_{ch-ag} represent the distance between neighbour cluster heads, cluster head to cluster member, cluster head to uncertain node and cluster head to agent

Notation	Definition
A_c	Work area of the NC-NET
$C = \{C_1, C_2, \cdots, C_m\}$	Set of NC-NET mobile nodes
$E = \{(i, j) \mid s(i, j) \leq 2R_c\}$	Set of wireless links
$C_{Msg} \in G$	Structure message of NC-NET nodes $C = (ID, HD, Type, XYcord, Nbn, CP, Nbs[])$
$Link_j^i(\tau)$	Signal links between node i and j at time τ
$Type_k^i$	Type of the node i in cluster $k, Type_k^i \in \{Memb, CH, agent, NR, toCH, toNR\}$
$R_{msg}(i)$	Maximum transmission range of node i
$R_c(i)$	Sensing radius of node i
$T_{life}(i)$	Lifetime of network sensor i

Table 1. Notation and definition in NC-NET.

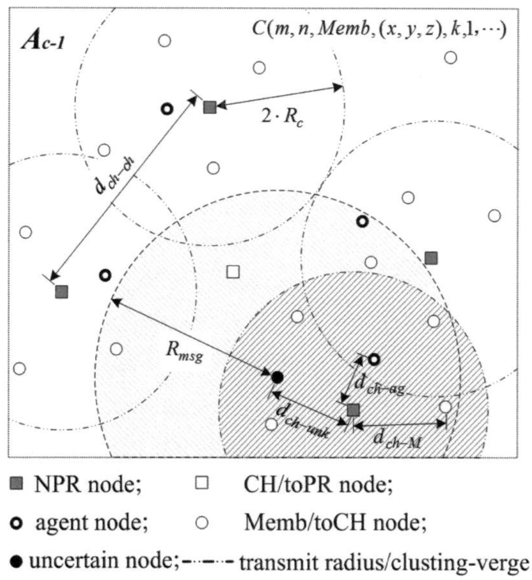

Figure 1. Sketch map of NC-NET model.

node, respectively. $2R_c$ is the cluster radius, and R_{msg} is the searching radius of uncertain node. Each interested grid has at least one sensor node within it, or the grid can be sensed by neighbour sensors.

2.2. Evaluating indicators

2.2.1. Coverage relevant model

Coverage is an important issue of ad hoc networks and is closely related to energy saving, connectivity and network reconfiguration [11–14]. The following is the main methods, which is adopted to assess coverage, comprising 3D *k*-coverage model and the necessary and sufficient condition (NSC) (**Table 2**).

Definition 1 (3D *k*-covered problem). Given a set of N sensors in area P, the radius of sensor node is R_c, if there is $C_{i1}, \ldots, C_{ik} \in \{C_1, \ldots, C_N\}$, $k \geq 1$. In this case, every position v in area P can meet the following formula.

$$v \in \bigcap_{j=1}^{k} \{x | dist(x, C_{ij}) \leq R_c\} \tag{2}$$

Then area P is 3D *k*-coverage by $\{C_1, C_2, \cdots, C_N\}$.

Theorem 1 is the necessary and sufficient condition used to determine the connected coverage set, which has been proved by Zhang and Hou in literature [23].

Theorem 1. Given a set of N sensors C in three-dimensional area P, $C = \{C_1, C_2, \cdots, C_N\}$, the communicating radius of sensor node is R_c; the sensing radius of sensor node is $R_c \geq 2R_s$.

Input: Sensing range R_s, maximum transmission range R_t, sensor nodes set V, and ε_0.

Output: $agent$, C_{CH}, C_{PR}.

```
for all u,v∈V(G), i∈NEW(G) do
while round==1//NC-NET initialization
C[v].{ID, Type} ←sensor[i].{PRI, Power}
Subprogram GetFirst_CHs();
end-while
while round==0//NC-NET regular circuit
if(C.new∩V(G)=Ø||C[i]∩V(G)=Ø)
Subprogram NEW_DEAD();
elseif(toCH[v]∪toAgent[v]≠Ø)
Subprogram RENEW_agent();
Subprogram RENEW_CHs();
CHs[v]←NEW_CHs[v]; AGs[v]←NEW_AGs[v];
end-if
CHs[u] ←CHs[v]; AGs[u] ←AGs[v];
CHs.{} ⇌ Ags.{};
BroadcastMsg(Ags[u].{ID,nbn,Level,CP});
BroadcastMsg(CHs[u].{ID,nbn,Level,CP});
while(toPR[v]≠Ø&round==0)
Subprogram RENEW_PRs();
BroadcastMsg(C[i].{ID,nbn,Level,CP})
end-while
BroadcastMsg(C[i].{ID,nbn,Level,CP});
end-for
```

Table 2. Main clustering procedure pseudo-code.

$\exists\ C_i \subset C$, $C_i = \{C_{i1}, \cdots, C_{ik}\}$. If sensing area of C_i can complete cover P, the set $C_i = \{C_{i1}, C_{i2}, \cdots, C_{ik}\}$ is a connected coverage set.

2.2.2. Link consumption indicator

Link quality is one of the key factors which affected the application of ad hoc network technique. In this chapter, we adopt tactical data link to extend it to solving the fleet-network-build-up problem, in which the following link consumption model is adopted.

In relatively short distances, the propagation loss problem is modelled as being inversely proportional to d^2, whereas for longer distance, it is inversely proportional to the propagation to d^4. Power control can be used to invert this loss by setting the power amplifier to ensure a certain power at the receiver [15–17]. Therefore, to transmit and to receive an l-bit packet in distance d, the radio expends the following energy, respectively:

$$E_{Tx}(l,d) = l \cdot E_{Tx\text{-}elec} + E_{Tx\text{-}amp}(l,d) = \begin{cases} l \times E_{elec} + l \times \varepsilon_{ft} \times d^2 & d < d_0 \\ l \times E_{elec} + l \times \varepsilon_{amp} \times d^4 & d \geq d_0 \end{cases} \tag{3}$$

$$E_{Rx}(l,d) = E_{Rx\text{-}elec}(l) = l \times E_{elec} \tag{4}$$

where d_0 is the free space model and multipath fading model. $E_{Tx\text{-}elec}$ is the electronics energy and depends on factors such as digital coding, modulation, and filtering of the signal before it is sent to the transmit amplifier. The parameters ε_{ft} and ε_{amp} depend on the required sensitivity and the noise figure of the receiver [12].

For the experiments described in this chapter, we adopted the parameters of the radio chips similar to those in [2] to determine the parameter values in (1) and (2). Then we have the representative values of the parameters ε_{amp} = 0.0013 pJ/bit/m^4, E_{elec} = 50 nJ/bit and ε_{ft} = 10 pJ/bit/m^2.

3. Distributed multi-weight data-gathering and aggregation protocol

In this section, we present the distributed multiple-weight data-gathering and aggregation protocol (DMDG) after describing the network model and evaluating indicator adopted, which consists of three parts as described in the following subsection.

3.1. Clustering algorithm

The hierarchical clustered sensor network is composed of a number of clusters. The following are some important definitions used in the clustering algorithm.

Definition 2 (Initial probability for cluster head)

$$p_{init} = \beta \cdot ID_i / ID_{\max} + (1-\beta) \cdot GDOP_i / GDOP_{\max} \tag{5}$$

where ID_i is the initial priority of sensor node i, $ID_{\max}$ is the maximum priority within the spherical radius r_c, $GDOP_i$ is the geometric distribution of position (GDOP) of sensor node i, $GDOP_{\max}$ is the optimum GDOP within the spherical radius r_c, and β is a self-adapting weighing factor.

Definition 3 (Electing factor for cluster head, EFCH)

$$W_i = \alpha \cdot \left(E_{ij} / \overline{E}^r \right) + (1-\alpha)/2 \cdot \frac{d_{\max} - d_{toBS}^i}{d_{\max} - d_{toBS}} + (1-\alpha)/2 \cdot GDP_k \tag{6}$$

where α is a self-adapting weighing factor, $\alpha = 1/(2+\beta)$, $(\beta = E_{ij}/\bar{E}^r)$. E_{ij} is the mean energy value of communicated consumption between sensor node C_i and other nodes in the same cluster,

$\bar{E}^r = E_{total}(r)/m$. d^i_{toBS} is the distance between C_i and cluster head node CH_k. d_{toBS} is the distance between CH_k and the cluster centre, $d_{toBS} = \sum_{i=1}^{m} d^i_{toBS}/m$. GDP_k is the GDOP of cluster head node CH_k.

Definition 4 (Correlation among sensor nodes). $\forall\ C_i, C_j \in G(V), \exists\ R(C_i, C_j) \in R^+, i \neq j$, if $\| D(C_i, C_j) \| \leq r$, $\| R(C_i, C_j) \| = 1$; else if $\| D(C_i, C_j) \| > r$, $\| R(C_i, C_j) \| = n + 1$, where n is the sensor number between C_i and C_j, r is the average 1-hop distance, and then $R(C_i, C_j)$ is called as the correlation between node C_i and C_j.

Now we describe our cluster formation algorithm in detail. The algorithm consists of three stages. In the initial stage, NC-NET nodes initiate the clustering procedure (Lines 2–5), round=1; NC-NCT nodes *sensor*[*i*] join into the network and obtain their own *ID*s and *Type*s, which are proportional to *PRI* and *power* of their link terminal; then run the subprogram *GetFirst_CHs*() to elect the first cluster head and agent, which is direct ratio to *ID* and *Type*.

When NC-NET is formed, round = 0, the program of regular circuit (Lines 7–21) will be performed. In the beginning of every cycle, cluster heads should judge whether there are new-coming requisitions *C.new* or new-dead node and judge whether there are new requisition for cluster head to *CH*[*v*] and for agent to *Agent*[*v*] and then execute relative treating subprograms *NEW_DEAD*(), *RENEW_agent*() and *RENEW_CHs*(), in which the first one is related to *ID*s and *Type*s and the last two subprograms are mainly determined by p_{init} and W_i which is defined in Definition 2 and Definition 3. When CHs[*i*] is selected as a cluster head, it broadcasts message *Msg*() to all other nodes to indicate its identity and adjust TDMA format. The agent and cluster head also communicate every cycle to back up information to preserve robustness and stability of the network. The procedure also handles the request for reference nodes *RENEW_PRs*() to realize renew of the network and assure load balance of the clustering protocol.

3.2. Data aggregation and communication scheme

This subsection presents the data aggregation mechanism and the communication mode among NC-NET nodes. The data transmitted among network members mainly has four portions, including the communication between reference nodes C_{PR} and cluster head C_{CH}, cluster head C_{CH} and the neighbour cluster head, cluster head C_{CH} and the cluster member C_{CM} and cluster member C_{CM} and the 2-hop neighbour node. Each transmission process has its own packet mode, including broadcast, data-centric, local transmission and multicast. The data packets have a unified scheme, main portions of which are shown in **Table 3**. Mainly composed of synchronous head, node's structural information C_{Msg}, sphere coordinate coefficient TS_{CA}, relative velocity V_C, heading angle φ_C and system time t_A. The received variables should accord with transmission demand and uniform formats, and the redundant information should be neglected.

- **NR-CH**: The data packet between reference node and cluster head node C_{CH} has three kinds of process: (i) the position reference nodes C_{PR} broadcast global coordinate information and the network distributing variable to cluster head nodes C_{CH}; (ii) the time reference

Packet	*head*	C_{Msg}	TS_{CA}	V_C	ϕ_C	t_A
NR-CH	√	√	√	–	√	√
CH-CH	√	√	–	–	–	√
CH-CM	√	√	√	–	–	√
CM-CM	√	√	–	√	√	–

Table 3. The format of data packet.

nodes C_{TR} broadcast system time t_A to C_{CH} and other network member; (iii) C_{CH} uploads its own sensing parameter and cluster member dynamic information to neighbour C_{PR}, which can be used for the next reference nodes' election.

- **CH-CH**: This transmitting process is to modify localization information for each other, which is used to define cluster verge. It is also used to acquire *ID* of neighbour cluster head node, which can be a relay node for multi-hop transmission.
- **CH-CM**: In this process, cluster head C_{CH} collects sensing information from its own cluster members C_{CM}, which is used for data aggregation and fusion. Then C_{CH} transmits system time t_A, transition matrix TS_{CA} and other information to C_{CM} under a TDMA channel sharing mechanism.
- **CM-CM**: In this process, cluster head C_{CH} broadcast sensing information to neighbour cluster heads in its own TDMA-based time slot. This information is mainly used to correct navigation parameters including position, velocity (or relative velocity) and heading angle. Other information is calculated into evaluating indicators, which are defined in Sections 2.2 and 3.1, for the next cluster head election.

3.3. Three-dimensional routing algorithm

When the network is clustered, specific methods for intra-cluster and intercluster communications depend on applications. For intra-cluster communication, the nodes can directly send data to the cluster head using time-division multiple-access (TDMA) schedule, just as in LEACH [7].

As shown in **Figure 2**, when node *B* broadcasts a packet, all the one-hop neighbours receive that packet. In order to avoid recipient ambiguity in a local broadcast, the incoming label of a node must be unique at least in its 2-hop neighbours. In the label assignment phase, the cluster head must execute an algorithm to ensure that each node is allocated a unique incoming label. A 3D heuristic routing algorithm is proposed for this purpose, which can be expatiated in the following example.

- **Step 1**: When node *A* receives the request packet from the node *B*, firstly, estimate whether the distance between nodes *B* and *A* (d_{AB}) satisfies the responding condition, $d_{AB} \leq 2 \cdot R_c$, and calculate the number of optimum hops (K_{hop}) if the condition is satisfied; if not, ignore the request. As shown in **Figure 2**, $K_{hop} = 3$.

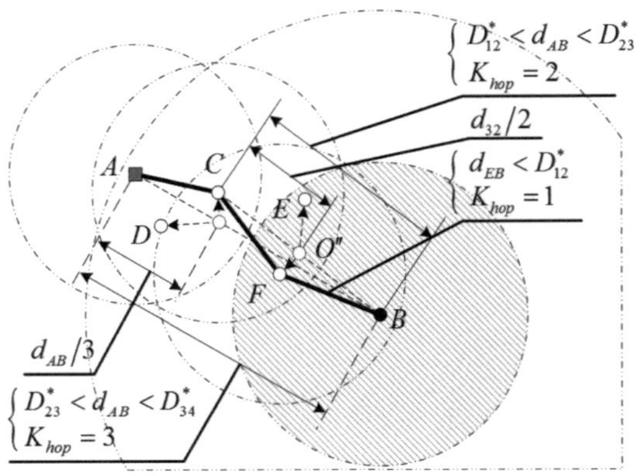

Figure 2. Geographic routing algorithm in NC-NET.

- **Step 2**: Node A computes the first trisection point O' between A and B based on geographic position got from the request packet, and then confirm point O' as the ideal next-hop position.
- **Step 3**: Node A compares all the distance between one-hop neighbour (nodes C and D) and point O'; then choose the next-hop node with the following equation, $Hop_i = \min_i \{|P_i - P_{opt}|\}$, in which i is ID of one-hop neighbours. So in the case of Step 2, the next-hop neighbour of node A is C, which obtains the information packet.
- **Step 4**: Node C repeats the steps (Steps (1)–(3)), and confirm the next-hop relay E, where $K_{hop} = 2$; then the node F obtains its next-hop relay B, where $K_{hop} = 1$. So the route is confirmed and the information transmitted through the route A-C-F to B; the routing procedure is finished.

4. Performance evaluation and simulation

To evaluate the performance of our scheme and compare it to both the association sponsor and central angle method, a set of simulations have been carried out, which are described in the following section.

4.1. Simulation setup

In our simulations, the NC-NET nodes are distributed schematically in a cubic region, and the number of nodes is varying from 5 to 50. In each simulation experiment, the deployment of sensor nodes is with a sparse setting and is in clusters based on DMDG. The default parameters used in both the simulations and the analysis are summarized in **Table 4**.

The proposed DMDG protocols were evaluated by extensive computer simulations by Matlab 2014 and compared with LEACH [7], DEEC and PEACH. The performance compared includes network lifetime, costs associated to clustering and backbone formation, as well as the

Parameters	Values
Network size (*Rcov,h*) (km)	20,2
The number of sensor nodes	5–50
Sensing range (*Rc*) (m)	5000 ~ 10,000
Maximum transmission range (*Rtmax*) (m)	15,000
Time interval for reporting data	30 s
MAC protocol	TDMA/CSMA
Radio frequency (MHz)	960 ~ 1206
E_{elec} in the energy model (μJ/bit)	1.16
d_0 in the energy model (km)	10
ε_{ft} in the energy model (pJ/bit/m^2)	10
ε_{amp} in the energy model (pJ/bit/m^4)	0.0013

Table 4. Main simulation parameters.

properties of generated clusters [19–24]. We assume that all the messages received from the cluster members can be aggregated into a single message.

Three kinds of scenarios are conducted in this simulation: (i) the average power consumption per node obtained by using LEACH, DEEC and DMDG; (ii) the lifetime and stable periods of the related LEACH, DEEC, PEACH and DMDG protocols; and (iii) the coverage rate versus proportion of dead nodes in different sensing range $R_c = 5, 8, 10$ km. We choose these scenarios because they are key factors in reflecting the efficiency of major technical points of DMDG protocol.

4.2. Performance result and analysis

As an addressing basic of the clustering process, it is critical to answer two questions before inspecting the proposed clustering protocol: (i) how does the number of nodes impact on the average power consumption, and (ii) how does the number of nodes impact on the average number of hops. The objective of the first scenario is to answer them through a simulation approach. **Figure 3** presents the average power consumption per node obtained by using LEACH, DEEC and DMDG and average number of hops versus the number of nodes when the maximum transmission range $R_{msg} = 15,000$ m, and the number of the node increase from 5 to 50.

It is clear in **Figure 3(a)** that DMDG always achieves the lowest power consumption and a relative stable hop number, $N_{hop} \approx 2$, which is gradually increasing in LEACH and DEEC. The average power consumption using DMDG can be as low as 0.637 when compared to LEACH and 0.824 when compared to DEEC. The stability in average number of hops results in stable of end-to-end delay; this can prove to be an advantage since it is convenient for estimating end-to-end delay and guarantee a data synchronism.

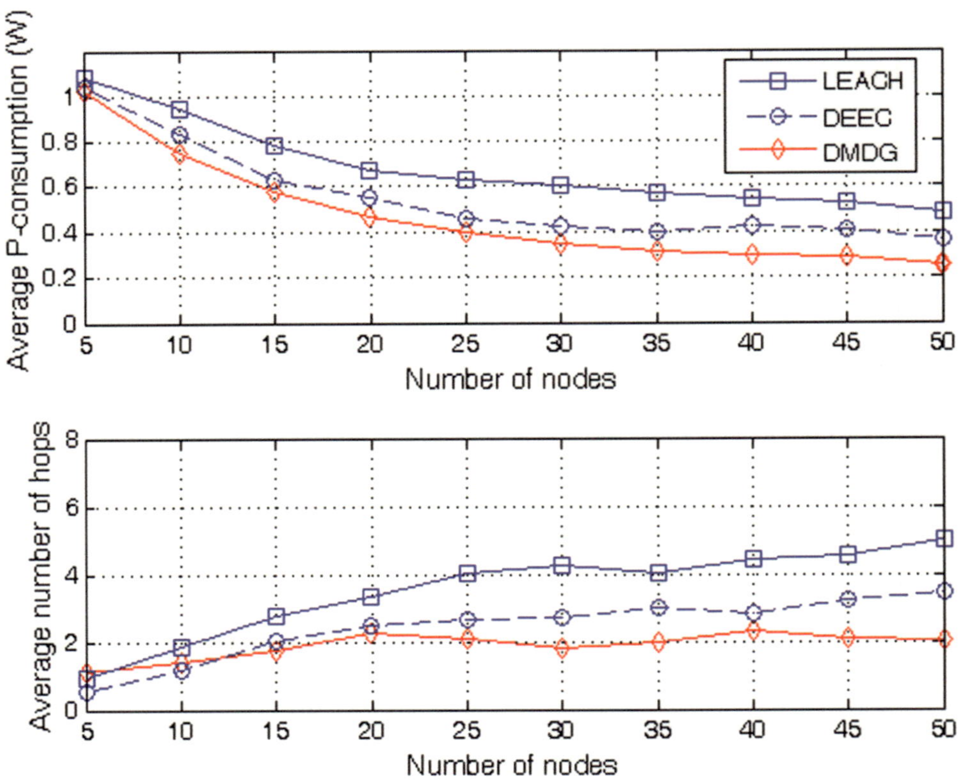

Figure 3. Average power consumption and average number of hops versus the number of nodes, N.

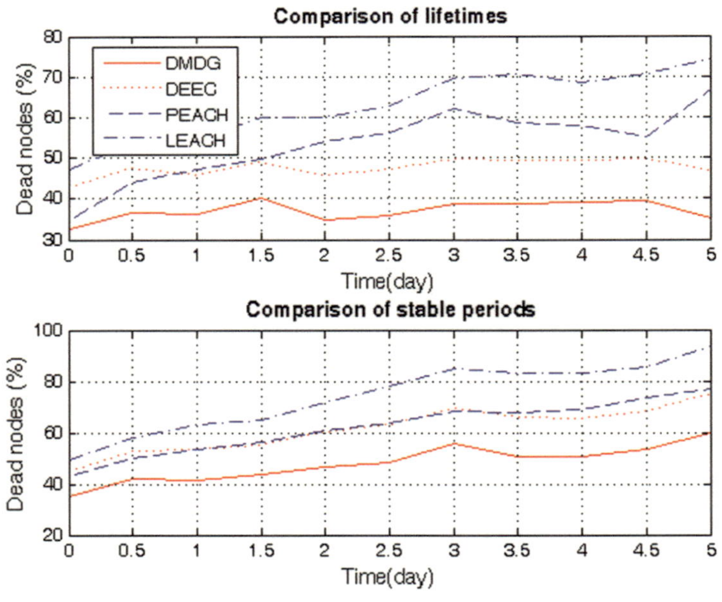

Figure 4. Comparison of lifetime and stable periods between LEACH, PEACH, DEEC and DMDG.

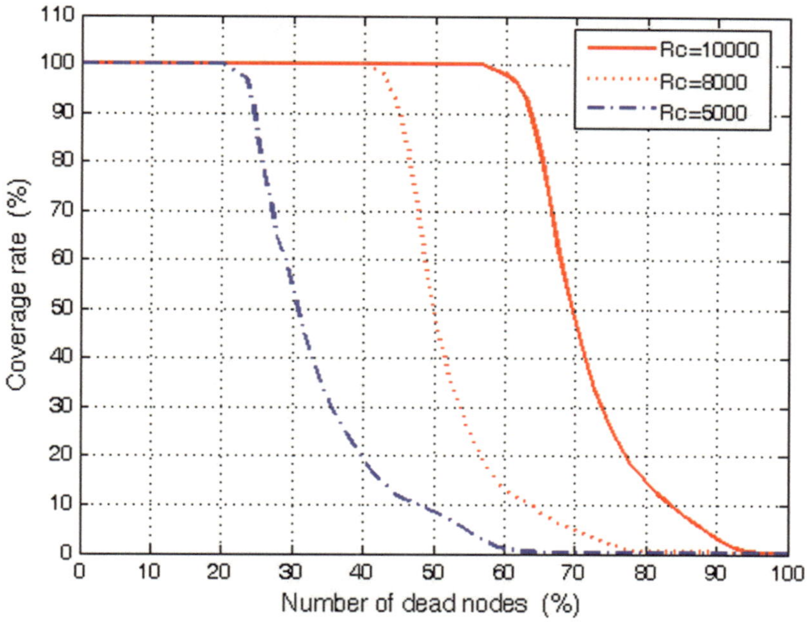

Figure 5. Coverage rate versus number of the dead nodes (R_c = 5, 8, 10 km).

Then, in the second scenario, we aim to investigate the lifetime and stable periods of the related LEACH, DEEC, PEACH and DMDG protocols, because the result is closely related with the topological balance of the NC-NET. The simulation results are presented in **Figure 4**. In the case of networks using DMDG with the maximum transmission range R_{msg} = 5000 m, the proportion of dead nodes (renew for mission) is 26% in lifetime and increases slowly in stable period (about 51% in the 4th day), which is much better than other protocols.

As the last scenario, we investigate the coverage rate performance with the increase of dead node, and the results are depicted in **Figure 5**. In this simulation, the coverage rate performance has been evaluated under three kinds of sensing range, that is, R_c = 5, 8, 10 km. The tendency curves of coverage rate have been compared with the increase of the number of dead node. Besides, DMDG protocol adopts the *3D*-coverage model, which is introduced in **Definition 1**, k = 2. The result has shown that DMDG can achieve a full two-coverage if the number of the dead nodes $n_{dead} \leq 11$ when R_c = 5 km, $n_{dead} \leq 20$ when R_c = 8 km and $n_{dead} \leq 29$ when R_c = 10 km; this conclusion approves that the DMDG protocol can guarantee a high-coverage environment in a fleet network with low-density in-motion nodes.

5. Conclusions

This chapter presented a new clustering and routing scheme, namely, the distributed multiple-weight data-gathering and aggregation protocol (DMDG), in order to work under long-distance sparse NC-NET and efficiently guarantee a long stable coverage rate through a unit circle test. Simulation results show that DMDG protocol can significantly extend the network lifetime when compared with other approaches. The NC-NET with DMDG protocol is equally applicable to the cases of three-dimensional localization and in-flight alignment for carrier-based aircraft. The detail performance evaluation of these cases will be resolved in the following research.

Acknowledgements

This chapter was supported in part by the National Natural Science Foundation of China under Grant no. 61473306 and partly by the Defence Advanced Research Project of China under Grant nos. 9140A09040614JB14001.

Author details

Chao Gao*, Guorong Zhao and Jianhua Lu

*Address all correspondence to: gaochao.shd@163.com

Department of Control Engineering, Naval Aeronautical and Astronautical University, Yantai, P.R. China

References

[1] Chong C. Y. and Kumar S. P. Sensor networks: evolution, opportunities and challenges. Proceedings of the IEEE. 2003;**91**(8):1247–1256.

[2] Gao C., Zhao G. R., Lu J. H., and Pan S. A grid-based cooperative QoS routing protocol with fading memory optimization for navigation carrier ad hoc networks. Computer Networks. 2015;**76**:294–316.

[3] Gao C., Zhao G. R., Lu J. H., and Liu T. Dynamic cooperative MAC protocol for navigation carrier ad hoc networks: a diffserv-based approach. International Journal of Antennas and Propagation. Forthcoming. 2016.

[4] Gao C., Zhao G. R., Lu J. H., and Pan S. Decentralised moving-horizon state estimation for a class of networked spatial-navigation systems with random parametric uncertainties and communication link failures. IET Control Theory and Applications. 2015;**9** (18):2666–2677.

[5] Lu J. H., Gao C., Zhao G. R., and Liu T. Decentralized state estimation for networked navigation systems with communication delay and packet loss: the receding horizon case. In: 17th IFAC Symposium on System Identification, Beijing, China. 2015. pp. 1094–1099.

[6] Gao C., Zhao G. R., and Pan S. DMDG: a distributed data-aggregation and routing protocol for fleet wireless sensor networks. In: The 2th International Conference on Inteligent Networks and Intelligent Systems, Tianjin, China. 2009. pp. 150–155.

[7] Soro S. and Heinzelman W. B. Cluster head election techniques for coverage preservation in wireless sensor networks. Ad Hoc Networks. 2008;**87**:955–972.

[8] Costa J. A., Patwari N., and Hero A. O. Distributed weighted-multidimensional scaling for node localization in sensor networks. ACM Transactions on Sensor Networks. 2006;**2** (1):39–64.

[9] Matrouk K. and Landfeldt B. KETT-gen: a globally efficient routing protocol for wireless sensor networks by equalizing sensor energy and avoiding energy holes. Ad Hoc Networks. 2008;**87**:514–536.

[10] Wahab O. A., Otrok H., and Mourad A. VANET QoS-OLSR: QoS-based clustering protocol for vehicular ad hoc networks. Computer Communications. 2013;**36**:1422–1435.

[11] Yi S., Heo J., and Cho Y. PEACH: power-efficient and adaptive clustering hierarchy protocol for wireless sensor networks. Computer Communications. 2005;**6**:2842–2852.

[12] Zhu X., Shen L., and Yum T. P. Hausdorff clustering and minimum energy routing for wireless sensor networks. IEEE Transactions on Vehicular Technology. 2009;**58**(2):990–996.

[13] Galluccio L., Leonardi A., and Morabitol G. A MAC/routing cross-layer approach to geographic forwarding in wireless sensor networks. Ad Hoc Networks. 2007;**16**:872–884.

[14] Jamal N., Al-Karaki J., and Ul-Mustafa R. Data aggregation and routing in wireless sensor networks: optimal and heuristic algorithms. Computer Networks. 2008;**36**:1–16.

[15] Boukerche A. and Fei X. A coverage-preserving scheme for wireless sensor networks with irregular sensing range. Ad Hoc Networks. 2007;**17**:1303–1316.

[16] Ren F., Dong S., and He T. A time synchronization mechanism and algorithm based on phase lock loop. Journal of Software. 2007;**18**(2):372–380.

[17] Cardei M. and Wu J. Energy-efficient coverage problems in wireless ad h13-420oc sensor networks. Computer Communications. 2006;**29**:413–420.

[18] Jin Y., Wang L., and Kim Y. EEMC: an energy-efficient multi-level clustering algorithm for large-scale wireless sensor networks. Computer Networks. 2008;**52**:542–562.

[19] Ang C. and Tham C. iMST: a bandwidth-guaranteed topology control algorithm for TDMA-based ad hoc networks with sectorized antennas. Computer Networks. 2008; **52**:1675–1692.

[20] Chang B. and Peng J. On the efficient and fast response for sensor deployment in sparse wireless sensor networks. Computer Communications. 2007;**30**:3892–3903.

[21] Yu Y., Xue X., and Wang X. Location discovery for three-dimensional sensor-actor networks using alternating combination quadrilateration. In: 6th International Conference on ITS Telecommunications Proceedings, Chengdu, China. 2006. pp. 1021–1024.

[22] Chuang S., Chen C., and Jiang C. Minimum-delay energy-efficient source to multilink routing in wireless sensor networks. Signal Processing. 2007;**87**:2934–2948.

[23] Zhang H. and Hou J. C. Maintaining sensing coverage and connectivity in large sensor networks. Ad Hoc & Wireless Networks. 2005;**1**(1):89–124.

[24] Ci S., Guizani M., and Sharif H. Adaptive clustering in wireless sensor networks by mining sensor energy data. Computer Communications. 2007;**30**:3235–3251.

[25] Le T., Hu W., and Corke P. ERTP: energy-efficient and reliable transport protocol for data streaming in wireless sensor networks. Computer Communications. 2009;**21**:3235–3251.

[26] Abbasi A. and Younis M. A survey on clustering algorithm for wireless sensor networks. Computer Communications. 2007;**30**:2826–2841.

Chapter 2

A Composite Trust Model for Secure Routing in Mobile Ad-Hoc Networks

Rutvij H. Jhaveri, Narendra M. Patel and
Devesh C. Jinwala

Additional information is available at the end of the chapter

http://dx.doi.org/10.5772/66519

Abstract

It is imperative to address the issue of secure routing in mobile ad-hoc networks (MANETs) where the nodes seek for cooperative and trusted behaviour from the peer nodes in the absence of well-established infrastructure and centralized authority. Due to the inherent absence of security considerations in the traditional ad-hoc routing protocols, providing security and reliability in the routing of data packets is a major challenge. This work addresses this issue by proposing a composite trust metric based on the concept of social trust and quality-of-service (QoS) trust. Extended from the ad-hoc on-demand distance vector (AODV) routing protocol, we propose an enhanced trust-based model integrated with an attack-pattern discovery mechanism, which attempts to mitigate the adversaries craving to carry out distinct types of packet-forwarding misbehaviours. We present the detailed mode of operations of three distinct adversary models against which the proposed scheme is evaluated. Simulation results under different network conditions depict that the combination of social and QoS trust components provides significant improvement in packet delivery ratio, routing overhead, and energy consumption compared to an existing trust-based scheme.

Keywords: packet-forwarding misbehaviour, secure routing, composite trust model, attack pattern discovery, mobile ad-hoc networks

1. Introduction

A mobile ad-hoc network (MANET) is an autonomous system of wireless mobile nodes that dynamically form a network in order to exchange information in the absence of centralized authority and fixed infrastructure. Mobile nodes communicate with each other in a multi-hop way to carry out data transmission due to limited communication range and resource constraints of the nodes. In the absence of router, each node operates as a host as well as a wireless router to forward packets for other nodes that may be outside its communication range [1]. The network functions well if all nodes operate in an altruistic manner. Due to the openness in network topology, distributed nature and lack of central authority, MANETs are particularly vulnerable to different types of routing attacks launched by internal nodes [2]. As a result, routing in such dynamic networks faces inherent challenges as compared to the traditional wireless networks. The traditional routing protocols proposed for ad-hoc networks are inefficient in dealing with different routing attacks.

The security schemes based on traditional cryptographic systems are typically used to resist external attacks. However, they prove to be inefficient in resisting the attacks launched by internal malevolent nodes. Such malicious nodes may seriously influence the security of the network by performing distinct types of packet-forwarding misbehaviours. In such a hostile environment, introducing the concept of 'trust' would provide prediction about the behaviour of neighbour nodes [2]. The notion of trust would prove to be useful for dynamic environments where the nodes need to depend on each other to achieve their goals [3]. Recently, trust management schemes have been considered as a viable security solution to improve the routing decisions in MANETs by detecting and isolating distrusted nodes [4].

In our previous work [5], we devised a trusted routing scheme with pattern discovery (TRS-PD) that integrates a trust model (based on QoS trust components) with an attack-pattern discovery mechanism in order to detect the malicious nodes earlier than a solitary trust model. TRS-PD estimates the distrust degree of neighbour nodes using direct trust computation. On the top of this, the attack-pattern discovery mechanism is introduced, which predicts suspicious activities of the neighbour nodes by promiscuously monitoring and recording specific fields of the control packets which are transmitted by the neighbour nodes. This gives an idea about the neighbour nodes, which might be following certain attack patterns. In addition, the scheme carries out indirect computation using recommendations by the trusted neighbours in order to enhance the trust establishment process. In this chapter, we propose enhanced TRS-PD (ETRS-PD), which uses a composite trust model that combines social trust component along with QoS trust components. ETRS-PD attempts to improve the packet delivery ratio against the adversary models discussed in Ref. [5] by enhancing the routing process. The performance of ETRS-PD is compared with TRS-PD against these adversary models under different network conditions.

The main technical contributions of this work are as follows: (1) An enhanced trust model is proposed for AODV protocol to evaluate neighbours' distrust value using composite trust metric. (2) Simulations carried out to compare the performance of ETRS-PD with TRS-PD prove that the performance of MANETs employing ETRS-PD is superior to that of MANETs employing TRS-PD against distinct types of adversaries.

The rest of the chapter is organized as follows. Section 2 discusses relevant related work. In Section 3, the proposed trust model is discussed. The enhanced trust-based on-demand routing scheme incorporated into AODV protocol is discussed in Section 4. Section 5 presents operations performed by various adversary models. The simulation results depicting the performance of ETRS-PD are presented in Section 6. Finally, Section 7 concludes the chapter.

2. Related work

A substantial amount of research work has been carried out in the last few years to address the security requirements of routing protocols by means of trust management.

A trust-based source routing (TSR) scheme devised by Xia *et al.* [6] attempts to discover a shortest secure route for data transmission in MANETs. Neighbour nodes are evaluated based on the historical trust values using correct packet-forwarding ratios. In addition, fuzzy logic is used to estimate a node's current trust based on its capability and historical trust value. This estimated value is used to predict the misbehaving nodes in the neighbourhood. A trusted route is selected for data transmission by avoiding such untrustworthy nodes. Experimental results show the effectiveness of TSR against blackhole, grayhole and modification attacks. However, the scheme incurs high computational overhead in calculation of route trust after arrival of every data packet at the destination. Furthermore, the scheme requires buffering of the packets in a circular queue, which incurs significant overhead in searching the match for the packets in the buffer. Gharehkoolchian *et al.* [7] proposed a novel trust model, which uses different *trust levels (TL)* for nodes and imposes the limitations based on the trust level in order to mitigate the malicious nodes. When a node enters the network, it is assigned $TL = 1$. It gains higher reputation if it acts normally by forwarding packets and thereby, it is assigned $TL = 2$. In case of malicious behaviour, it is assigned $TL = 0$. If the malicious behaviour of the node is observed for three times, it is assigned $TL = -1$ and the node is permanently blocked. During the route discovery process, when a node receives a route reply from its neighbour node, it verifies its *TL* value. If the node is a non-malicious node ($TL = 2$), the route reply is forwarded. Otherwise, a test route request is sent to the suspicious node ($TL = 1$) after the received route reply. If an abnormal reply is received from the suspicious node in response to the test route request, the route reply is discarded after assigning $TL = 0$ to the node and the node is blocked for a specific time. Thus, the scheme attempts to isolate the malicious nodes during route discovery process. However, it does not have any reactive mechanism to cope up with sudden drops in packets during data transmission phase; instead, it just detects the adversary but attempts to isolate it during the next route discovery process. Airehrour *et al.* [8] proposed *GradeTrust* protocol to isolate blackhole adversaries by selecting a secure path, in addition to elimination of excessive routing computations and minimization of communication overhead. It classifies the nodes into three sets in order of the trust levels: *Trusted Friends, Friends* and *Possible Friends*. Trust level is assigned by monitoring neighbours' request packet-forwarding ratio. A source node selects the next hop from its Trusted Friends, and the process continues until the packet reaches the destination. In the case of unavailability of a Trusted Friend, a Friend is selected. A compromised node is dissociated swiftly from other trusted nodes, and it is pushed down to the lower trust level. However, the scheme does not consider the forwarding ratio of data packets in calculation of the trust level, which makes it susceptible to packet dropping adversaries during data transmission phase. In addition, simulation results showing comparison of the proposed protocol with the traditional protocols are not promising. Patel *et al.* [9] proposed a trust model for AODV-based MANETs, which attempts to increase network lifetime by uniform consumption of energy. A trust value is computed based on dropping ratios and delays of control and data packets as well as residual node energy. The scheme attempts to discover a trusted route during the route reply propagation towards the source node on the reverse path. All the intermediate nodes receiving the route reply packet update the path trust value in the packet using the available trust values of neighbours. If a node receives multiple route reply packets, it compares the trust of the newly received path with that of the current path and stores the path with the maximum trust value. However, the scheme does not have any reactive mechanism to fight against packet-dropping adversaries during data transmission phase. After identifying an adversary, it waits for the next route discovery process to isolate it. Chiejina *et al.* [10] proposed a solution to evaluate the trust of a node in the network, which ensures that nodes expending their energy in forwarding data and control packets for other nodes are allowed to carry on their activities while the malevolent nodes are isolated from the network. Trust values are computed by direct observations, which are aggregated at different time intervals to provide a historical reputation of the node. The total reputation value of a node is mapped with a grading criterion to decide the status of a node. Nodes with lower reputation value than the set threshold value are blacklisted and denied the network resources. Routes containing blacklisted nodes are discarded, and alternative routes are discovered. The solution attempts to mitigate selfish and deceitful nodes from the network with scarce resources. However, whenever the source sends a packet towards the destination, the solution generates additional overhead as *path administrator* has to check that the packet has not been sent via a path containing a blacklisted node. Mylsamy *et al.* [11] proposed a *preference-based protocol for trust and head selection (2PTH)*, which takes four parameters to calculate a trust value: packet delivery ratio, packet misrouting ratio, packet alteration ratio, and packet injection ratio. Depending on the affected security parameters, weighing coefficients' values are determined. Trust values are classified into three different categories: high, medium and low. If trust value of a node goes below its relative threshold, it is not allowed to participate as a cluster member. A cluster-based routing mechanism is used which discovers a stable cluster head based on external factors such mobility, connectivity and distance as well as internal factors such as residual battery power, processing power and memory. When a cluster head of the cluster of the destination node receives a route request packet during the route discovery process, it verifies the trustworthiness of the node in order to establish a secure route. Simulation results show promising performance of the protocol as compared to some existing protocols. However, the protocol does not have any reactive mechanism for identifying packet-dropping adversaries during data transmission phase. Moreover, *weight assignment* and *cluster head election* consume a significant amount of computational resources. Indirani *et al.* [12] presented a *swarm-based distributed intrusion detection system (SDIDS)* with the objective to remove the complexity in the design of an IDS caused by the inherent MANET characteristics. Active nodes in a route are selected by *ant colony optimization (ACO)* technique based on a node's packet-forwarding activities, residual bandwidth, residual energy and connectivity. A *forward ant* reaches to every node in order to compute and update the pheromone value using the aforementioned parameters. When it reaches the destination, the information collected by the forward ant about all the hops is transferred to the *backward ant*. The backward ant then traverses on the reverse path and reaches to the source in order to deliver the status of all nodes. A routing decision is then made by selecting the optimal route to the destination. However, the scheme incurs high computational overhead in calculation of route trust. In addition, establishment of a trusted route should not be the sole responsibility of the source node. Xia *et al.* [13] proposed a *light-weight trust-enhanced routing protocol (TeAOMDV),* which attempts to provide an optimal two-way trusted route without containing the malicious entities. Its trust framework uses passive and local monitoring information to evaluate the trust values of neighbours. It considers activity, stability and historical trust record of a node in evaluation of a node trust. Moreover, the trust value is modified by collecting the recommendations from the trusted neighbours. It uses *hop count, forward path trust* and *reverse path trust* as the metrics to compose a three-dimensional evaluation vector for taking routing decisions. The authors extend their work by proposing an improved *SCGM(1,1)-Markov chain prediction method* based on the *system cloud grey model* and *Markov stochastic chain theory* to forecast trust level of a node for future routing decisions. However, it holds similar drawbacks as the scheme proposed in [12] due to the consideration of route trust. Azer *et al.* [14] proposed a new reputation system for ad hoc networks, called *misbehaviour detection and control (MDAC),* which encourages the nodes to act in a trustworthy manner. It obtains first hand and second hand information about neighbouring nodes. Trust is evaluated based on number of incoming packets and total consumed time to deliver packets. The *MDAC modeller module* combines all collected information about a node into a meaningful reputation value. Based on the reputation values, nodes in the network are guided to take necessary actions such as trust/don't trust, cooperate/don't cooperate and forward/don't forward. A node is considered eligible for service only after verifying its reputation value. The mechanism shows better performance compared to an existing scheme in terms of throughput and delay. However, the mechanism does not consider control packets in the calculation of the reputation value which delays the detection of sequence number attacks. In addition, it adds significant computational overhead in making reputation decisions about neighbouring nodes. Rajkumar *et al.* [15] proposed a trust-based light-weight authentication routing protocol which adopts multipath route discovery technique to mitigate adversaries. A route is rated based on packet success rate after route reply is forwarded to the source node. An optimal path for data transmission is chosen based on its rating, and the next optimal path is stored as an alternative arrangement. The protocol calculates a trust value using *EigenTrust* algorithm, which is based on direct and indirect observations of neighbour nodes. A resolver is engaged for computing a global trust value of the node, which also executes trust noise cancellation mechanism. If the trust value of a node goes below the threshold value, it is authenticated using the *Shamir's secret sharing* technique. If a node is found to be malicious, all routes going through the node are discarded and the alternate optimal path is selected. However, cryptographic approaches add considerable amount of communication and memory overhead along with key distribution issues. In addition, the scheme involves high computational overhead in the estimation of packet success rate and calculation of the global trust value.

3. Trust model

As a part of the literature survey, we discover that a composite trust metric based on social and QoS trust components may successfully perform tasks to meet both performance and trust requirements [16, 17]. We have noticed some work in the literature moving in this direction.

Cho *et al.* [17] considered honesty and intimacy, while Kohlas *et al.* [18] considered honesty, competency, reliability and maliciousness as social trust components to define trust relationships. In addition, we observe that *energy consumption* is an important QoS trust component for improving the network performance [17, 19]. Taking these notes into consideration, we devise an enhanced trust-based scheme, *ETRS-PD*.

ETRS-PD considers *ditch ratio* as a social trust component in estimation of distrust degree of the neighbours. This social trust component is utilized to know the magnitude of misbehaviour carried out by a node while residing in monitoring node's neighbourhood. In addition, *energy consumption* is considered as an additional QoS component along with *packet drop ratio*. Thus, a composite trust metric is constructed by including social trust along with QoS trust. Furthermore, the routing process of TRS-PD is modified to enhance the routing decisions. As aforementioned, ETRS-PD attempts to improve the packet delivery ratio against the adversary models discussed in our previous work [5].

In our trust model, we compute historical trust on a constant basis after a specific time interval called trust update interval. Overall, our trust model performs trust derivation and trust computation along with discovery of attack patterns. We modify the trust model of TRS-PD to perform trust derivation and trust computation in a different way.

3.1. Basic assumptions

Our trust-based scheme makes the following assumptions: (i) all the mobile nodes have identical physical characteristics; (ii) the wireless links in the network are bidirectional; (iii) all the nodes operate in promiscuous mode in order to observe the neighbour nodes and (iv) the source and the destination are benevolent nodes. The above assumptions are fulfilled by wireless MAC layer protocols.

3.2. Trust derivation

Our proposed trust model uses direct observations to derive distrust values of neighbour nodes by observing packet dropping ratios, energy consumption and ditch ratio of neighbour nodes. In addition to this, each node employs an attack pattern discovery mechanism, which detects malicious patterns generated by neighbour nodes in the transmitted control packets. We also consider recommendations of trusted neighbours for improving the routing decisions.

3.3. Trust computation

In a routing process, neighbour node's distrust is evaluated by the sender by observing activities carried out by that neighbour. To be specific, a node n_i will increase the distrust score of its neighbour n_j if the n_j does not forward the packet sent by n_i [5].

Definition 1. *Control dropping ratio (CDR)*: It is the ratio of the number of control packets dropped to the number of control packets which are supposed to be forwarded. At time *t*, *CDR(t)* is computed as follows:

$$CDR(t) = \frac{NC_d(t)}{NC_a(t)} \tag{1}$$

where *NCd(t)* signifies the cumulative count of dropped control packets, and *NCa(t)* represents the total number of sent control packets from time *0* to *t*.

Definition 2. *Data dropping ratio (CDR)*: It is the ratio of the number of data packets dropped to the number of data packets, which are supposed to be forwarded. At time *t*, *CDR(t)* is computed as follows:

$$DDR(t) = \frac{ND_d(t)}{ND_a(t)} \tag{2}$$

where *NDd(t)* signifies the cumulative count of dropped control packets, and *NDa(t)* represents the total number of sent control packets from time *0* to *t*.

Definition 3. *Energy consumption (EC)*: It is the ratio of the energy consumed by a node to the initial energy of that node. When a node possesses limited residual energy, it may not hold the capabilities to forward the packets of other nodes. At time *t*, *EC(t)* is computed as follows:

$$EC(t) = \frac{EI - ER(t)}{EI} \tag{3}$$

where *EI* signifies the initial energy, and *ER(t)* signifies the residual energy of the node at time *t*.

Definition 4. *Ditch ratio (DTR)*: It is the ratio of the number of times a neighbour node is found to be distrusted while receiving its *HELLO* packets to the total number of *HELLO* packets received from that node. At time *t*, *DTR(t)* is computed as follows:

$$DTR(t) = \frac{NH_d(t)}{NH_a(t)} \tag{4}$$

where *NHd(t)* signifies the number of times a distrusted neighbor node has ditched the monitoring node while sending *HELLO* packets, and *NHa(t)* signifies the total number of *HELLO* packets received from that neighbour node.

The obtained distrust value of a node *nj* by a monitoring node *ni* is the measure of packet dropping activities, energy drain rate and magnitude of misbehaviour. The distrust value of node *nj* evaluated by node *ni*, denoted as *DTVij*, is calculated by the following formula:

$$DTV_{ij}(t) = w1 \times CDR_{ij}(t) + w2 \times DDR_{ij}(t) + w3 \times EC_{ij}(t) + w4 \times DTR_{ij}(t) \tag{5}$$

where $w1$, $w2$, $w3$ and $w4$ ($w1, w2, w3, w4 \geq 0$ and $w1 + w2 + w3 + w4 = 1$) are the weights assigned to *CDR*, *DDR*, *EC* and *DTR*, respectively.

In our trust model, distrust values are restricted in the range from 0 to 1 (i.e., $0 \leq DTVij \leq 1$). The distrust value 0 indicates complete trust, whereas the distrust value 1 signifies complete distrust. We set the initial value of distrust to 0 as we assume all the nodes to be benevolent initially. Meanwhile, the distrust value constantly varies with the time as per the behaviour of neighbour nodes. We use a distrust threshold η to differentiate the malicious nodes from benign nodes.

As discussed in Ref. [5], we incorporate an attack pattern discovery mechanism on the top of the trust model, which employs the model of *method of common differences (MCD)*. Thus, the pattern discovery mechanism attempts to identify the adversaries following attack patterns prior to conducting misbehaviours; on the other hand, the trust model detects other packet-dropping adversaries during the trust update procedure.

4. Enhanced trust-based on-demand routing

While any reactive routing protocol can be extended to incorporate ETRS-PD, we extend ad-hoc on-demand distance vector (AODV) protocol for this purpose. In addition to the modifications described in [5], we further modify the functionality of AODV in order to improve the routing decisions. The neighbour table is modified by appending the following fields: (i) *Energy consumption,* (ii) *Ditch count:* The number of times a neighbour node is found to be distrusted while receiving its *HELLO* packets, (iii) *HELLO count:* The total number of *HELLO* packets received from a neighbour node and (iv) *Ditch ratio*. The *distrust value* is calculated as per the formula (5). We modify the *HELLO* packets to include an additional field: (i) *Energy consumed*: Energy consumed by the node, which is provided as information to the neighbour nodes (calculated as per the formula (3)).

4.1. Routing strategy

We further modify the routing strategy described in Ref. [5]. The modified routing strategy (by modifying *Step 4*, *Step 8* and *Step 9*) is described herewith:

Step 1: Before starting data transmission, the source node *ns* looks up in its local routing table for the destination node n_d.

Step 2: If entry exists, it starts sending data through the trusted next hop to n_d. Go to *Step 8*.

Step 3: If no such route exists, n_s initiates a route discovery process by flooding route request (RREQ) packets to discover a route to n_d.

Step 4: When an intermediate node n_k receives a route reply (RREP) from its neighbour node n_j, it accepts the reply only if n_j is not a distrusted node (n_k finds absence of attack patterns for n_j with distrust value less than or equal to η) and *recommended as a trusted node.*

Step 5: If multiple route replies are received after the route discovery process, a route entry for the route with the highest destination sequence number and trusted next hop is created for *nd* and inserted into the routing table of *ns*.

Step 6: If no such route is discovered, go to *Step 3*.

Step 7: Node n_s starts data transmission to *nd*.

Step 8: If an intermediate node n_k finds a next hop n_m distrusted (*by direct observation or by recommendation*) in its routing table for a destination n_p during the trust update procedure, the entry is discarded. A local route discovery process is initiated by n_k to discover an alternate route to n_p.

Step 9: Even though an intermediate node *nk* finds a distrusted neighbor n_m attempting to regain its trust by recuperating the distrust value less than or equal to η, *it is still considered as a distrusted node* (i.e. it is *not* reconsidered as a trusted node).

4.2. Routing procedures

The procedures for sending RREQ, receiving RREQ and sending RREP remain unmodified as presented in **Figures 1–3**, respectively (as described in Ref. [5]).

```
Algorithm 1: SendRREQ( )                //By the source node

Fill up RREQ packet with the required fields
Broadcast the RREQ packet to discover route to the destination
```

Figure 1. *SendRREQ* procedure [5].

```
Algorithm 2: ReceiveRREQ( )             //By the destination node or an intermediate node

If (The received RREQ is duplicate) then
  Discard the RREQ
Else
  If (New or updated route is found) then
    Update the routing table entry for the source node
    Construct or update reverse route towards the source node
  End If
  If (The receiving node is either the destination or intermediate node with fresher route) then
    SendRREP( )
  Else
    Record the required field values from the received RREQ for SL2
    Update necessary fields in the RREQ before rebroadcasting
    Rebroadcast the RREQ packet
  End If
End If
```

Figure 2. *RecvRREQ* procedure [5].

```
Algorithm 3: SendRREP( ) //By destination/intermediate node having fresher route

If (Sending node is the destination node) then
  Increment the destination sequence number
End If
Fill up RREP packet with the required fields
Unicast the RREP packet on the reverse route towards the source
```

Figure 3. *SendRREP* procedure [5].

The modifications carried out in the receiving RREP procedure are highlighted in **Figure 4**.

```
Algorithm 4: ReceiveRREP( ) //By intermediate node on the reverse route or source node

Record the required field values from the received RREP (or from the overheard RREP)
Insert the corresponding recorded values into SL1 and SL2
If (The neighbor sending RREP is marked as distrusted or recommended as distrusted) then
   Discard the RREP
Else
   If (New or updated route is found) then
      Update the routing table entry for the destination node
   End If
   If (Receiving node is the source node) then
      Discard the RREP
      Send data through the forward route if the route is fresher and next hop is trusted
   Else
      Forward the RREP packet on the reverse route towards the source
   End If
End If
```

Figure 4. *RecvRREP* procedure.

The procedure for route maintenance remains unmodified as presented in **Figure 5** (as described in Ref. [5]).

```
Algorithm 5: MaintainRoute( )                //By each node

If (A link is broken) then
   If (The route is active and the destination is within the maximum hop limit) then
      Initiate local route repairing
   Else
      Carry out required updates in routing table
      Notify upstream nodes about the broken link by sending RERR containing unreachable destinations
   End If
End If
If (RERR is received) then
   Carry out required updates in the routing table
   If (Receiving node is the source node) then
      Re-initiate route discovery process
   Else If (The route is active and the destination is within the maximum hop limit) then
      Initiate local route repairing
   Else
      Rebroadcast the RERR packet
   End If
End If
```

Figure 5. *Route maintenance* procedure [5].

4.3. Trust update and trust recommendation procedures

The modifications carried out in the trust update and trust recommendation procedures are highlighted in **Figures 6** and **7**, respectively.

```
Algorithm 6: UpdateTrust( )                    //By each node

For (Each neighbor table entry)
Do
    Verify the existence of attack patterns from SL1 and SL2 of the neighbor
    Calculate DTV value of the neighbor
      If (The neighbor follows attack patterns or has DTV > η) then
        Mark the node as a distrusted node
      Else If (The neighbor is not marked as a distrusted node and recommended as
            a trusted node) then
        The node remains as a trusted node
      End If
Done
For (Each routing table entry)
Do
   Find the entry of the next hop from the neighbor table
   If (The next hop is found to be distrusted or recommended as distrusted in the neighbor
      table) then
        Discard the route containing the malevolent next hop
        Initiate a local route discovery process to discover an alternate route to the destination
   End If
Done
```

Figure 6. *Update trust* procedure.

```
Algorithm 7: RecommendTrust( )              //By each node

//Before broadcasting a HELLO packet//
Construct an empty Blacklist for recommendation purpose
For (Each neighbor table entry)
Do
   If (The neighbor is marked as a distrusted node) then
     Insert the neighbor identity into the Blacklist
   End If
Done
Incorporate the Blacklist and Energy Consumption information into the HELLO packet
Broadcast the HELLO packet to the neighbors
//After receiving a HELLO packet//
Receive HELLO packet from the neighbor
Enter the Energy Consumption information of the neighbor into the neighbor table
If (The neighbor sending the HELLO packet is trusted) then
  Obtain the Blacklist from the HELLO packet
  For (Each entry in the Blacklist)
  Do
    Find the corresponding entry in the neighbor table
    If (The neighbor entry exists) then
      Set Recommendation value as 'distrusted' for the neighbor
    End If
  Done
End If
```

Figure 7. *Recommend trust* procedure.

5. Adversary models

It is obvious that the success of any security mechanism largely depends on the operations performed by the adversaries. In our work, we evaluate the performance of ETRS-PD against three adversary models described in Ref. [5].

5.1. Intelligent adversary model

The operations performed by *intelligent adversary* (denoted as *Attack1*) are presented in **Figure 8** [5, 20]. The adversary follows a pattern in inserting the value of hop count (Hop_Count = 2) while sending RREP packet.

```
Procedure 1: Actions by the malicious node to learn the routing information in promiscuous mode

If (RREQ or RREP packet is received or overheard) then
   Update the information in the routing table
   If (Highest_Recorded_Dest_Seqno < Dest_Seqno in the received/overheard packet) then
      Highest_Recorded_Dest_Seqno = Dest_Seqno in the received/overheard packet
   End If
End If

Procedure 2: Actions by the malicious node after receiving an RREQ

Discard the received RREQ
If (RREQ is NOT for me) then
   If (valid fresher route is available in the routing table) then
      Fill up RREP with Dest_Seqno=Incremented value of
                        Highest_Recorded_Dest_Seqno and Hop_Count=2
      Unicast the forged RREP on the reverse path to the source
   End If
Else
   Fill up RREP with own Seqno and Hop_Count=1
   Unicast the genuine RREP on the reverse path to the source
End If

Procedure 3: Actions by the malicious node after receiving a data packet from the source node

If (data packet is NOT for me) then
   Time1=Receipt time of the first data packet
   Time2=time1+50% of the Total life time
   If (Time2 > Total life time) then
      Time2=Total life time
   End If
   If (Current Time ≥ time1 && Current Time ≤ time2) then
      Drop the data packet received from the source
   Else
      Forward the data packet
   End If
Else
   Receive the data packet for me
End If
```

Figure 8. Operations performed by a node launching *Attack1* [5, 20].

5.2. Slow poison adversary model

The operations performed by *slow poison adversary* (denoted as *Attack2*) are presented in **Figure 9** [5]. The adversary follows a pattern in inserting the value of destination sequence number (RREQ_Dest_Seqno + 1) while sending RREP packet.

```
Procedure 1: Actions by the malicious node after receiving an RREQ

If (RREQ is NOT for me) then
   If (route is available in the routing table) then
      Fill up RREP with Dest_Seqno=RREQ_Dest_Seqno+1 and Hop_Count=Random(1,2)
      Discard the received RREQ
      Unicast the forged RREP on the reverse path to the source
   Else
      Discard the received RREQ
   End If
Else
   Fill up RREP with own Seqno and Hop_Count=1
   Unicast the genuine RREP on the reverse path to the source
End If

Procedure 2: Actions by the malicious node after receiving a data packet from the source node

If (data packet is NOT for me) then
   Calculate the current time slot count i=int(Current_Time/10)
   Packets_to_be_dropped= Fibonacci(i)                    // fi= fi-1+fi-2
   If (Total_packets_dropped_in_current_time_slot < Packets_to_be_dropped) then
      Drop the data packet received from the source
      Increment the value of Total_packets_dropped_in_current_time_slot
   Else
      Forward the data packet
   End If
Else
   Receive the data packet for me
End If
```

Figure 9. Operations performed by a node launching *Attack2* [5].

5.3. Capricious adversary model

The operations performed by *capricious adversary* (denoted as *Attack3*) are presented in **Figure 10** [5]. This adversary does not generate any attack pattern while sending RREP packet.

```
Procedure 1: Actions by the malicious node after receiving an RREQ

Discard the received RREQ
If (RREQ is NOT for me) then
   If (valid fresher route is available in the routing table) then
      Fill up RREP with Dest_Seqno=Routing_table_Dest_Seqno+Random(1,7)
                     and Hop_Count=Random(1,3)
      Unicast the forged RREP on the reverse path to the source
   End If
Else
   Fill up RREP with own Seqno and Hop_Count=1
   Unicast the genuine RREP on the reverse path to the source
End If

Procedure 2: Actions by the malicious node after receiving a data packet from the source node

If (data packet is NOT for me) then
   If (Packet_ID mod Random(1,3) == 0) then
      Drop the data packet received from the source
   Else
      Forward the data packet
   End If
Else
   Receive the data packet for me
End If
```

Figure 10. Operations performed by a node launching *Attack3* [5].

6. Simulation results and analysis

NS-2 (ver. 2.34) simulator is used to evaluate the performance efficiency of ETRS-PD against the three adversary models, namely *Attack1, Attack2* and *Attack3*. To prove our claim that ETRS-PD provides enhanced routing process than our previous proposal, TRS-PD [5], the performance of ETRS-PD is compared with TRS-PD against all three adversary models. We employ IEEE 802.11 MAC to carry out simulations in an area of 1000 × 1000 m. The benign nodes were randomly distributed over the network, which employs either AODV, ETRS-PD or TRS-PD protocol. Randomly positioned malicious nodes selectively perform packet forwarding misbehaviours by employing either of the three adversary models, namely *Attack1, Attack2* and *Attack3*. It is considered that the wireless network interface consumes 1.65, 1.4, 1.15 and 0.045 W for the *Transmit, Receive* and *Idle* modes and the *Sleep* state, respectively [21]. We take 800 μs as the transition time from the Sleep state to Awake state and during this transition period, a mobile node will consume 2.3 W power. All the experimental data are obtained after performing 10 different simulations and taking their average values. The major simulation parameters are shown in **Table 1**.

Parameter	**Value**
Coverage area	1000 × 1000 m
MAC layer protocol	IEEE 802.11
Communication range of each node	250 m
Channel bandwidth	2 Mbps
Traffic type	CBR-UDP
Packet size	512 bytes
Mobility model	Random way point
Simulation duration	240 s
Number of nodes	50
Maximum mobility (varying)	4–20 m/s
Pause time	5 s
Number of connections	15
Percentage of malicious nodes (varying)	0–40%
Routing protocols	AODV, *Attack1, Attack2, Attack3*, TRS-PD, ETRS-PD
Initial energy	1000 J
Transmit power	1.65 W
Receive power	1.4 W
Idle power	1.15 W
Sleep power	0.045 W
Transition power	2.3 W
Transition time	800 μs

Table 1. Simulation parameters.

In order to evaluate the performance of ETRS-PD, the following performance metrics are used: *packet delivery ratio (PDR)*, *normalized routing overhead (NRO)* and *average energy consumption (AEC)*. The following network parameters are varied: (1) *maximum speeds of nodes* and (2) *percentage of adversaries*.

The performance of AODV and TRS-PD in terms of PDR and NRO is already evaluated in Ref. [5], while their performance in terms of AEC is evaluated in Ref. [21].

6.1. Test 1: varying node mobility

In this test, the performance of the protocols is evaluated against *Attack1*, *Attack2* and *Attack3* by varying mobility of nodes from 4 to 20 m/s and keeping other parameters fixed. The percentage of malicious nodes is kept fixed to 20% for all three types of adversaries.

As shown in **Figure 11**, the PDR of AODV under *Attack1* declines from nearly 46 to 39% as the mobility increases from 4 to 20 m/s. The increase in packet loss at higher mobility is due to the increased number of link breakages at higher node speeds. Meanwhile, PDR of AODV under *Attack2* and *Attack3* declines from nearly 68 to 60% and 74 to 64%, respectively, as shown in **Figures 12** and **13**, respectively. When TRS-PD is employed, the PDR declines from nearly 73 to 57%, 79 to 69% and 80 to 69% under *Attack1, Attack2* and *Attack3,* respectively. This considerable rise in PDR is due to the integration of the attack-pattern discovery mechanism with the trust model. Meanwhile, when ETRS-PD is employed, it provides improvement in PDR over TRS-PD by an average of 6.21 under *Attack1*, 2.82 under *Attack2* and 4.03 under *Attack3*. The reasons behind improved results are as follows: (i) Construction of a composite trust metric using social trust and QoS trust. (ii) Enhanced routing decisions due to the modifications carried out in receive RREP, trust update and trust recommendation procedures.

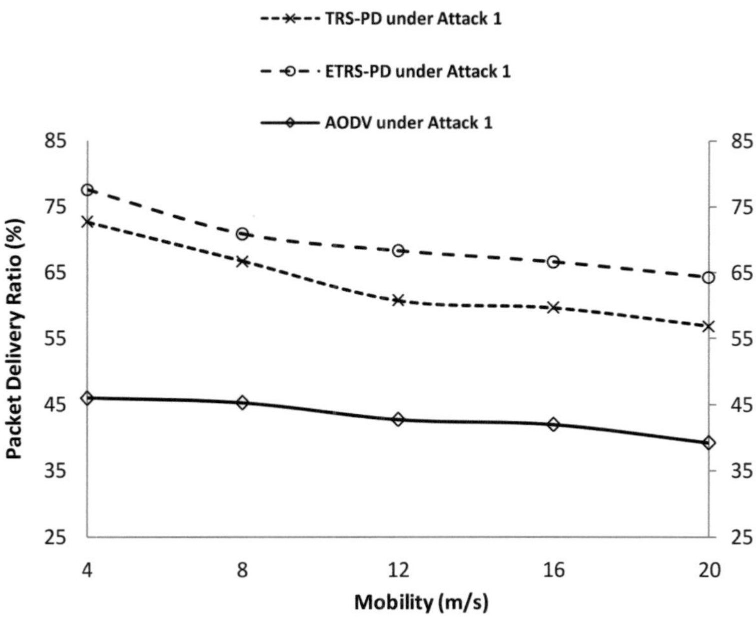

Figure 11. PDR under *Attack1*.

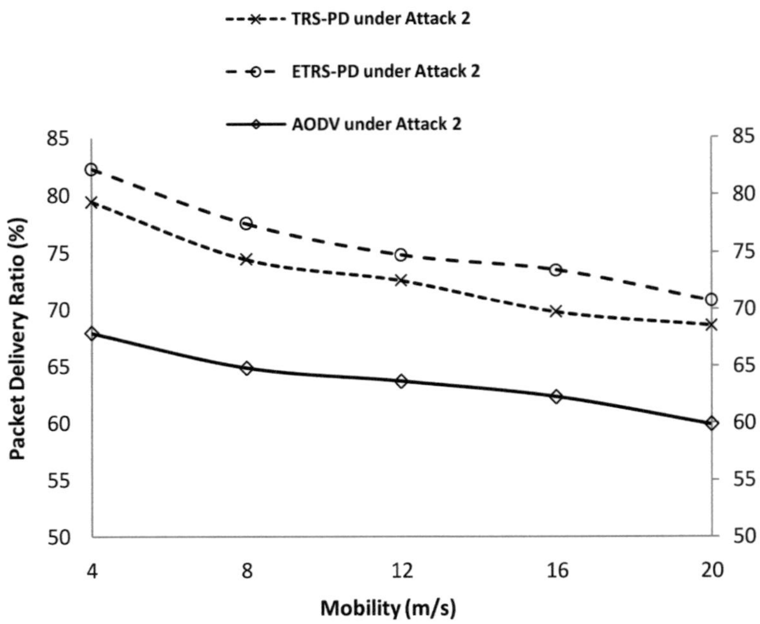

Figure 12. PDR under *Attack2*.

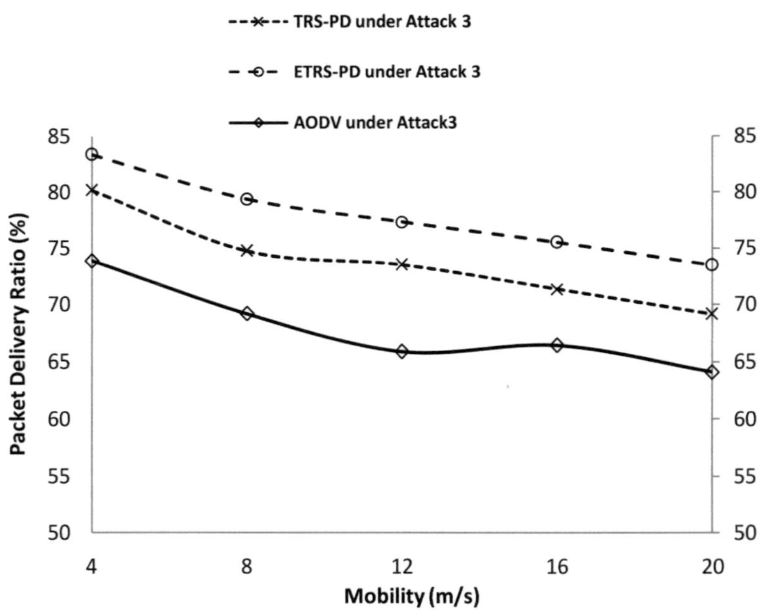

Figure 13. PDR under *Attack3*.

As shown in **Figures 14–16**, as the node speed increases, the NRO of AODV increases from nearly 5.7 to 10.4, 1.8 to 4.1 and 2.8 to 5.1 under *Attack1*, *Attack2* and *Attack3*, respectively.

Meanwhile, the TRS-PD provides improved performance over AODV by providing NRO from nearly 4.5 to 8.5 and 2.8 to 5.1 under *Attack1* and *Attack3*, respectively. On the other hand, due to the *Fibonacci dropping behaviour* of *Attack2* during the data transmission phase, the number of route hand-off mechanisms increases for TRS-PD as time goes on. As a result, resultant NRO is higher than that of AODV, which varies between nearly 3.2 and 5.5. Meanwhile, ETRS-PD provides improvement in NRO over TRS-PD by an average of 1.43 under *Attack1*, 0.30 under *Attack2* and 0.36 under *Attack3*. The reason behind this is, ETRS-PD leads to less number of route hand-off mechanisms than TRS-PD due to the inclusion of two more components in the overall trust composition as well as enhanced routing process.

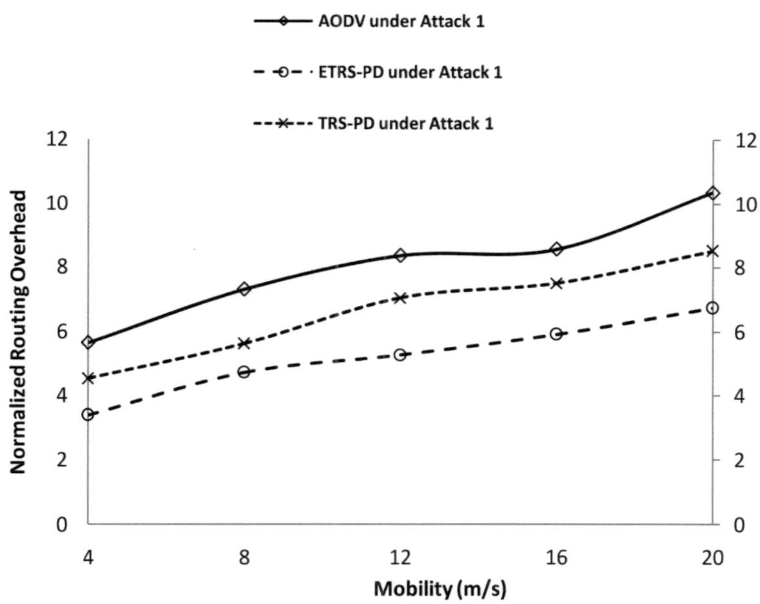

Figure 14. NRO under *Attack1*.

In order to ensure the improvement in energy consumption, we compare the performance of ETRS-PD with TRS-PD. As depicted by the graph in **Figure 17**, the AEC under *Attack1* varies between 313.56 and 314.13 J when employing TRS-PD. Meanwhile, ETRS-PD improves the AEC of TRS-PD by an average of 1.6 J. As depicted by the graph in **Figure 18**, the AEC under *Attack2* varies in the range of 312.82–314.4 J when employing TRS-PD. Meanwhile, ETRS-PD improves the AEC of TRS-PD by an average of 0.57 J. As depicted by the graph in **Figure 19**, the AEC under *Attack3* varies between 312.79 and 313.41 J when employing TRS-PD. Meanwhile, ETRS-PD improves the AEC of TRS-PD by an average of 0.57 J.

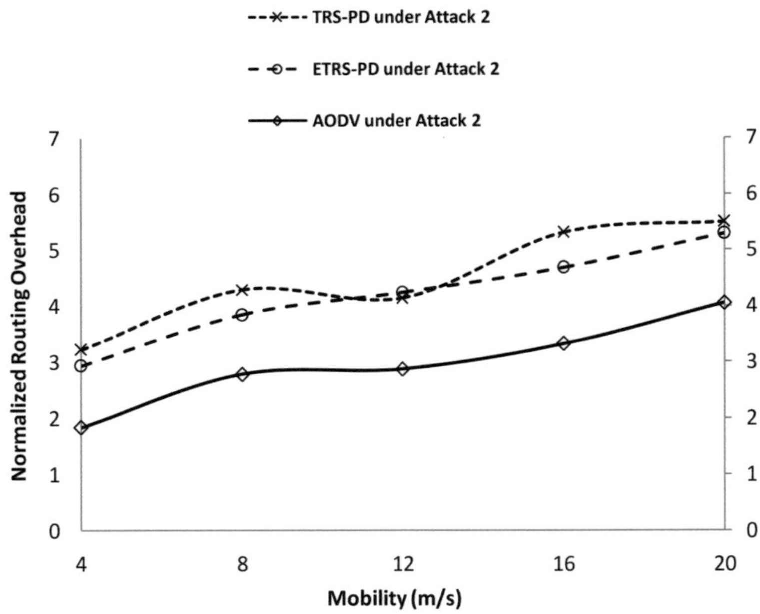

Figure 15. NRO under *Attack2*.

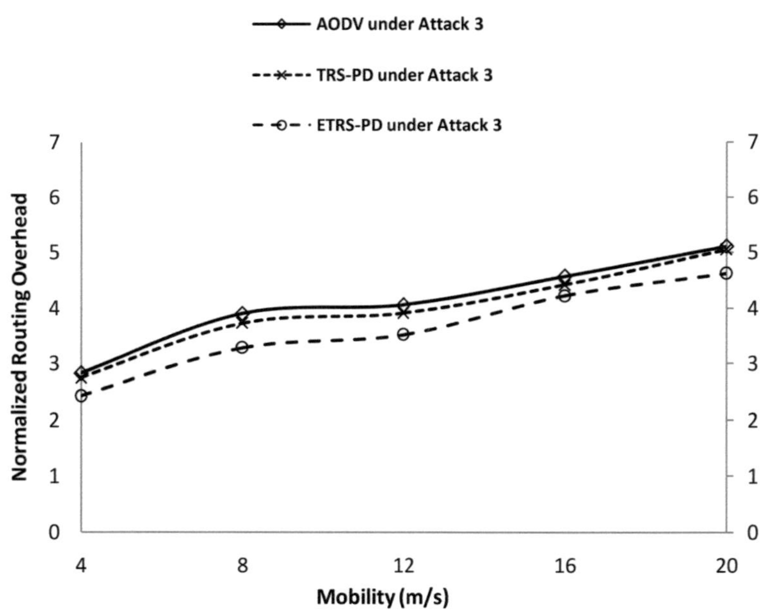

Figure 16. NRO under *Attack3*.

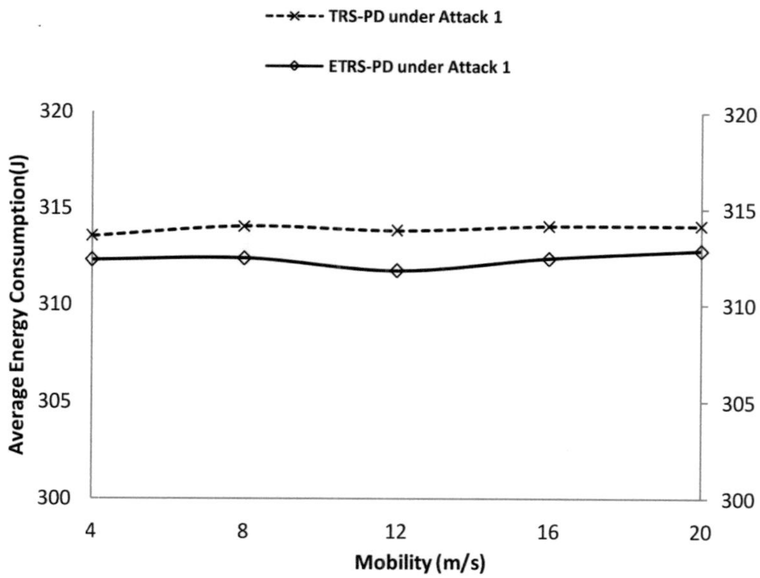

Figure 17. AEC under *Attack1*.

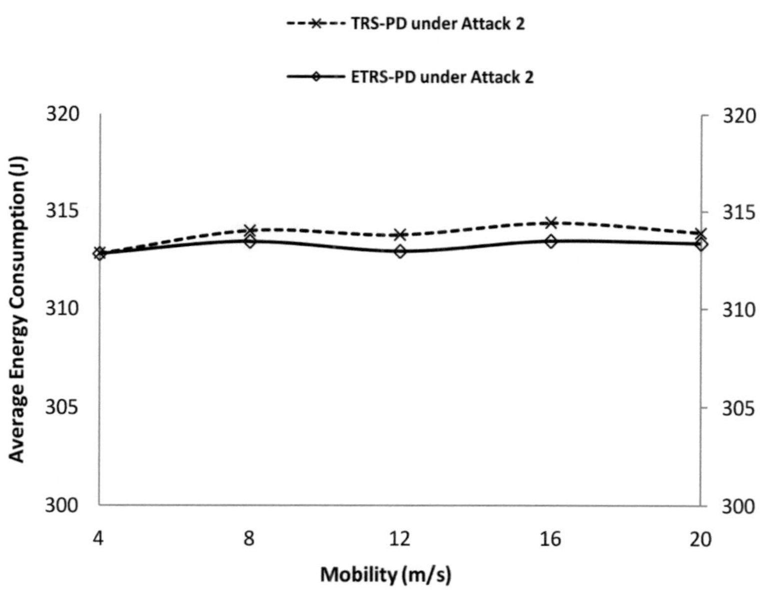

Figure 18. AEC under *Attack2*.

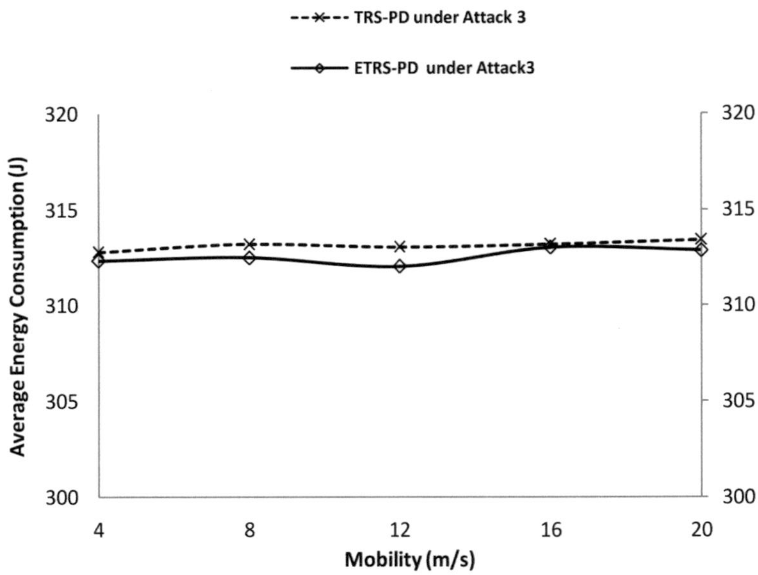

Figure 19. AEC under *Attack3*.

6.2. Test 2: varying percentage of malicious nodes

In this test, the performance of the protocols is evaluated against *Attack1*, *Attack2* and *Attack3* by varying percentage of malicious nodes from 0 to 40% and keeping other parameters fixed. The mobility parameter is kept fixed to 20 m/s for all three types of adversaries.

As shown in **Figures 20–22**, due to the increased intensity of packet dropping activities with the percentage increase in malicious nodes, the PDR of AODV declines from nearly 79 to 32%, 79 to 54% and 79 to 56% under *Attack1*, *Attack2* and *Attack3*, respectively. On the other hand, TRS-PD proves provides improvement in PDR of nearly 12 to 18%, 8 to 9% and 4.5 to 7% in the presence of malicious nodes launching *Attack1*, *Attack2* and *Attack3*, respectively. Meanwhile, in the presence of adversaries, ETRS-PD provides improvement in PDR over TRS-PD by an average of 7.67 under *Attack1*, 2.14 under *Attack2* and 4.29 under *Attack3*.

The NRO of AODV varies in the range of nearly 4.8–12.1, 3.9–4.8 and 4.7–5.4 under *Attack1*, *Attack2* and *Attack3*, respectively, as shown in **Figures 23–25**. On the other hand, TRS-PD improves NRO by maximum of 2.2 and 0.5 under *Attack1* and *Attack3* respectively over AODV. Meanwhile, TRS-PD increases NRO from nearly 0.7 to 2.0 under *Attack2* as compared to AODV. On the other hand, in the presence of adversaries, ETRS-PD provides improvement in NRO over TRS-PD by an average of 2.22 under *Attack1*, 0.25 under *Attack2* and 0.46 under *Attack3* due to the aforementioned reasons.

As shown in **Figures 26–28**, when employing TRS-PD, the AEC of the network without the presence of adversaries is 313.84 J while that is 312.35 J when employing ETRS-PD. As shown in **Figure 26**, the AEC for the MANET employing TRS-PD under *Attack1* varies between 314.08

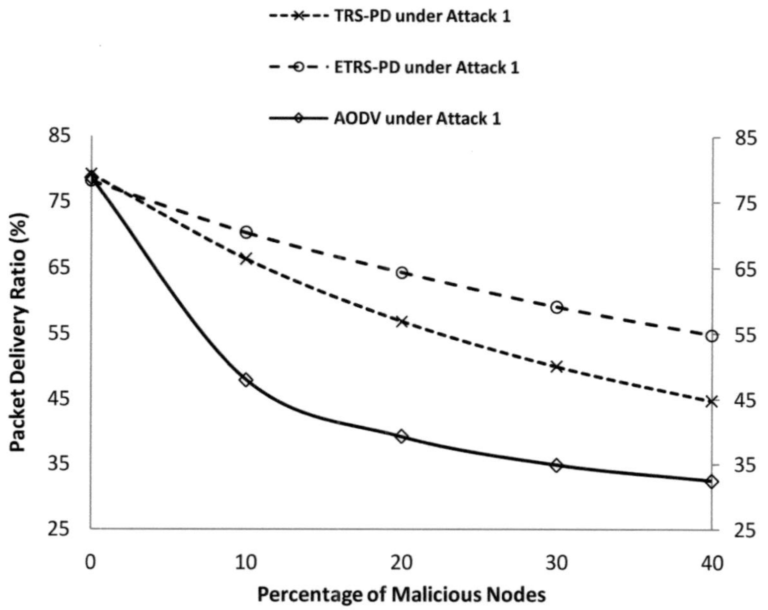

Figure 20. PDR under *Attack1*.

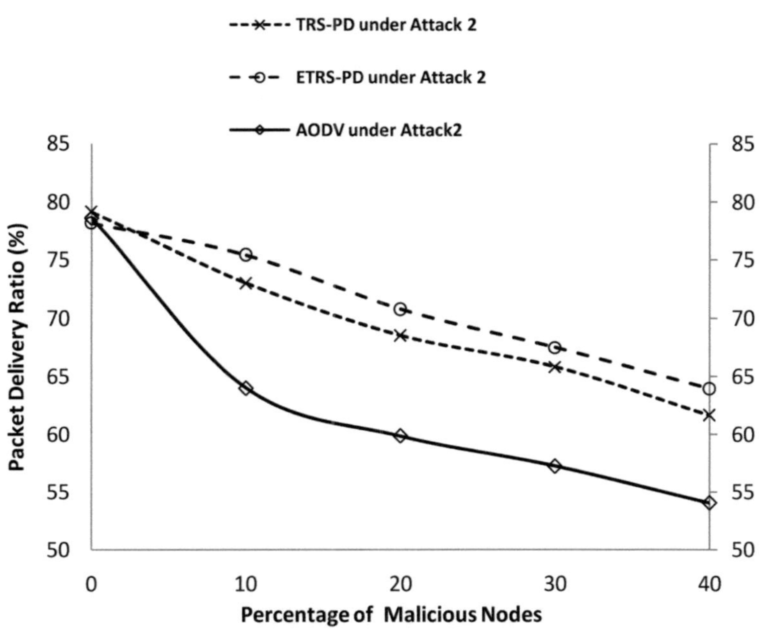

Figure 21. PDR under *Attack2*.

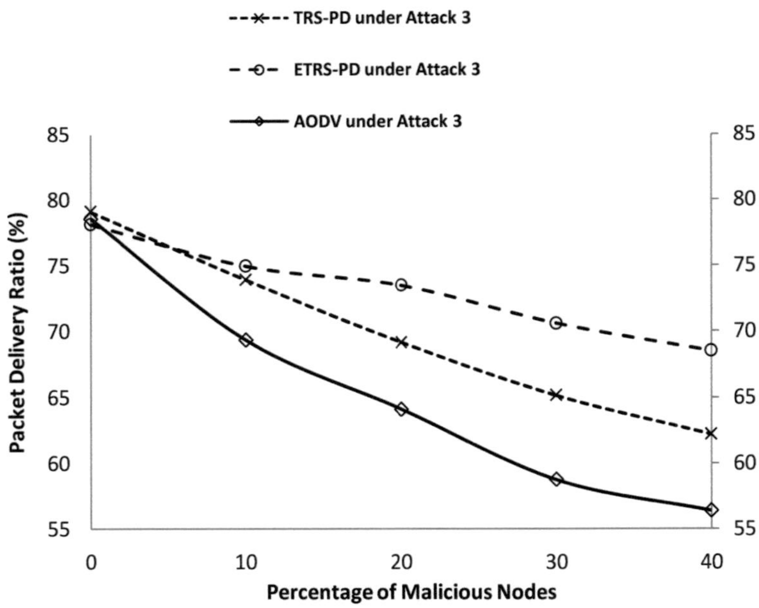

Figure 22. PDR under *Attack3*.

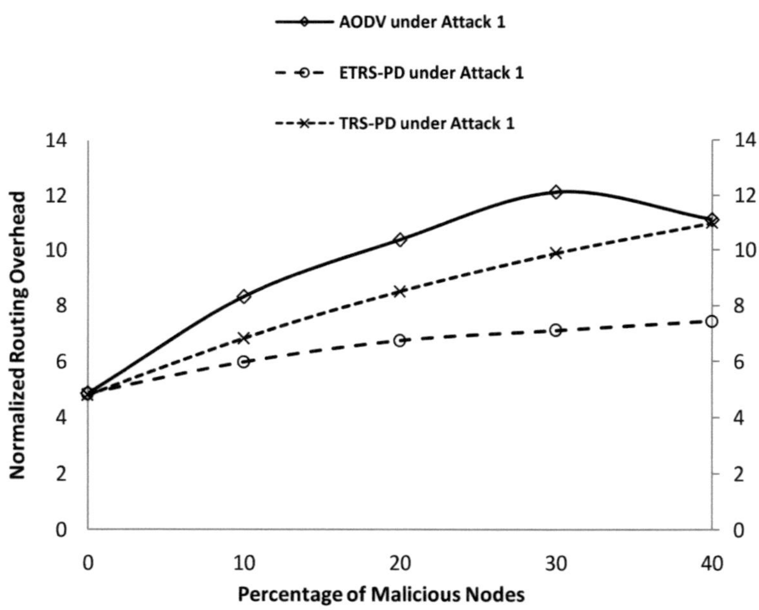

Figure 23. NRO under *Attack1*.

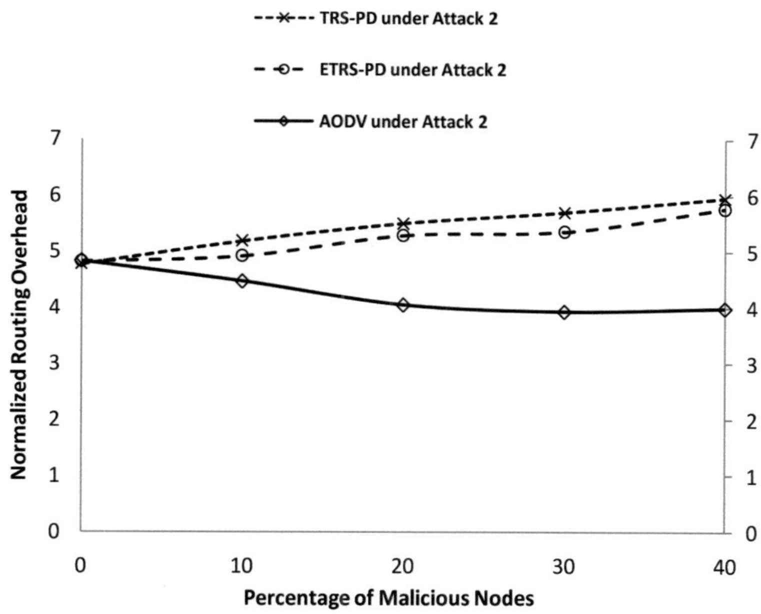

Figure 24. NRO under *Attack2*.

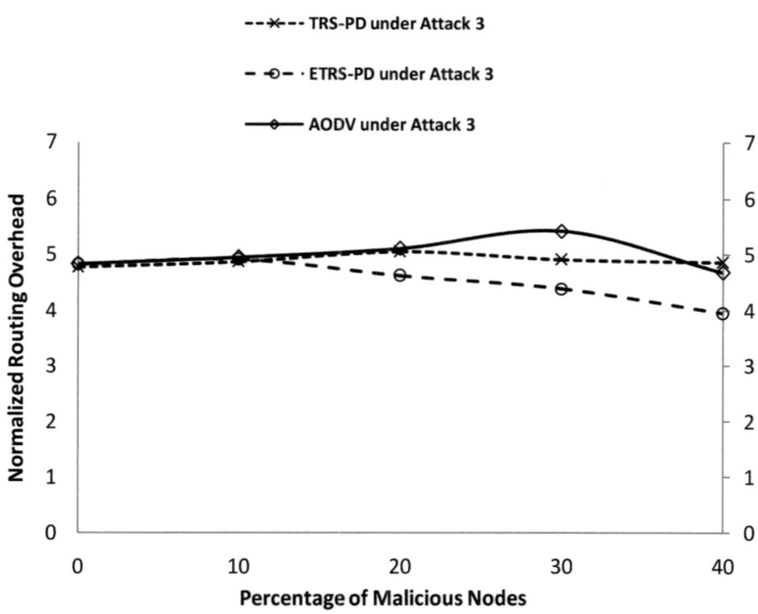

Figure 25. NRO under *Attack3*.

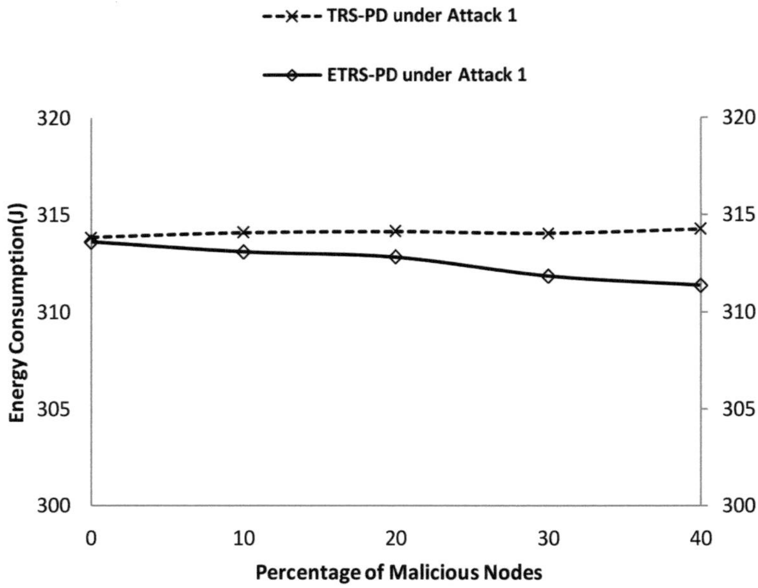

Figure 26. AEC under *Attack1*.

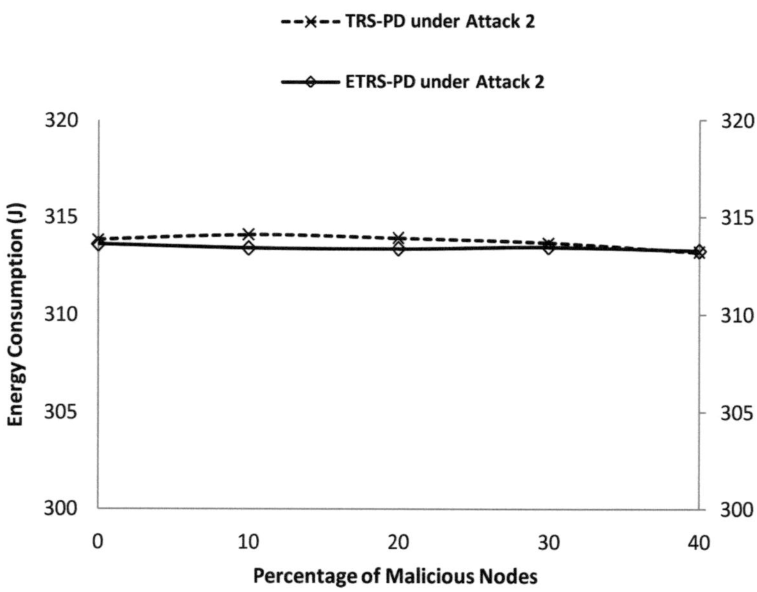

Figure 27. AEC under *Attack2*.

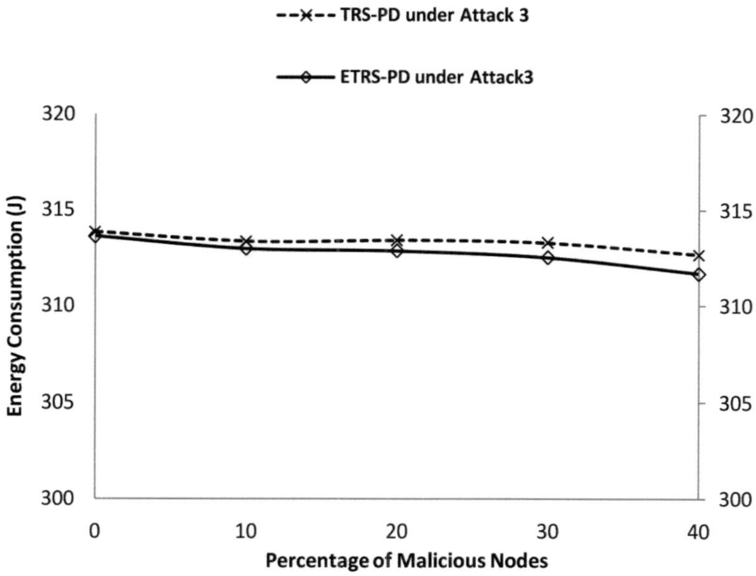

Figure 28. AEC under *Attack3*.

and 314.25 J. Meanwhile, ETRS-PD improves the AEC of TRS-PD by an average of 1.83 J in the presence of adversaries. As shown in **Figure 27**, the AEC of the MANET employing TRS-PD under *Attack2* decreases from 314.08 to 313.2 J. Meanwhile, ETRS-PD improves the AEC of TRS-PD by an average of 0.34 J in the presence of adversaries. As shown in **Figure 28**, the AEC of the MANET employing TRS-PD under *Attack3* varies between 312.68 and 313.41 J. Meanwhile, ETRS-PD improves the AEC of TRS-PD by an average of 0.67 J in the presence of adversaries.

7. Conclusions

As a part of the literature survey, we observe that integration of QoS trust and social trust in the composition of a trust metric would improve the performance of a trust-based scheme. Considering these notes, we modify our previous trust-based scheme, TRS-PD, such that it combines both the types of trust components. In addition, we suggest modifications in the route discovery, trust update and trust recommendation procedures of TRS-PD. The proposed trust-based approach, ETRS-PD, improves the routing decisions due to the suggested modifications. The performance comparison of ETRS-PD with TRS-PD under three distinct adversary models shows that ETRS-PD achieves remarkable improvement in packet delivery ratio due to the enhanced routing process and inclusion of two new trust components. Moreover, ETRS-PD reduces the generation of number of control packets due to the reduced number of route hand-off mechanisms. As a result, ETRS-PD provides improved normalized routing overhead as well as energy consumption as compared to TRS-PD under different network scenarios.

Author details

Rutvij H. Jhaveri[1]*, Narendra M. Patel[2] and Devesh C. Jinwala[3]

*Address all correspondence to: rhj_svmit@yahoo.com

1 SVM Institute of Technology, Bharuch, India

2 Birla Vishvakarma Mahavidyalaya, V.V. Nagar, India

3 Sardar Vallabhbhai National Institute of Technology, Surat, India

References

[1] Junhai, L., Danxia, Y., Liu, X. and Mingyu, F. A survey of multicast routing protocols for mobile ad-hoc networks. IEEE Communications Surveys & Tutorials. 2009;**11**(1):78–91.

[2] Xia, H., Jia, Z., Ju, L., Li, X. and Sha, E.H.M. Impact of trust model on on-demand multi-path routing in mobile ad hoc networks. Computer Communications. 2013;**36**(9):1078–1093.

[3] Yu, H., Shen, Z., Miao, C., Leung, C. and Niyato, D. A survey of trust and reputation management systems in wireless communications. Proceedings of the IEEE. 2010;**98**(10):1755–1772.

[4] Marchang, N. and Datta, R. Light-weight trust-based routing protocol for mobile ad hoc networks. IET Information Security. 2012;**6**(2):77–83.

[5] Jhaveri, R.H. and Patel, N.M. Attack-pattern discovery based enhanced trust model for secure routing in mobile ad-hoc networks. International Journal of Communication Systems. 2016; DOI: 10.1002/dac.3148.

[6] Xia, H., Jia, Z., Li, X., Ju, L. and Sha, E.H.M. Trust prediction and trust-based source routing in mobile ad hoc networks. Ad Hoc Networks. 2013;**11**(7):2096–2114.

[7] Gharehkoolchian, M., Hemmatyar, A.A. and Izadi, M. Improving security issues in MANET AODV routing protocol. In: International Conference on Ad Hoc Networks; Springer International Publishing; 2015. pp. 237–250.

[8] Airehrour, D., Gutierrez, J. and Ray, S.K. Gradetrust: a secure trust based routing protocol for MANETs. In: International Telecommunication Networks and Applications Conference (ITNAC); IEEE; 2015. pp. 65–70.

[9] Patel, V.H., Zaveri, M.A. and Rath, H.K. Trust based routing in mobile ad-hoc networks. Lecture Notes on Software Engineering. 2015;**3**(4):318–324.

[10] Chiejina, E., Xiao, H. and Christianson, B. A dynamic reputation management system for mobile ad hoc networks. Computers. 2015;**4**(2):87–112.

[11] Mylsamy, R. and Sankaranarayanan, S. A preference-based protocol for trust and head selection for cluster-based MANET. Wireless Personal Communications. 2016;**86**(3): 1611–1627.

[12] Indirani, G. and Selvakumar, K. A swarm-based efficient distributed intrusion detection system for mobile ad hoc networks (MANET). International Journal of Parallel, Emergent and Distributed Systems. 2014;**29**(1):90–103.

[13] Xia, H., Yu, J., Tian, C.L., Pan, Z.K. and Sha, E. Light-weight trust-enhanced on-demand multi-path routing in mobile ad hoc networks. Journal of Network and Computer Applications. 2016;**62**:112–127.

[14] Azer, M.A. and Saad, N.G.E.D. A new reputation system for misbehavior detection and control in ad hoc networks. In: International Computer Science and Engineering Conference (ICSEC); IEEE; 2015. pp. 1–6.

[15] Rajkumar, B. and Narsimha, G. Trust-based light weight authentication routing protocol for MANET. International Journal of Mobile Network Design and Innovation. 2015;**6**(1):31–39.

[16] Cho, J.H., Swami, A. and Chen, R. A survey on trust management for mobile ad hoc networks. IEEE Communications Surveys & Tutorials. 2011;**13**(4):562–583.

[17] Cho, J.H., Swami, A. and Chen, R. Modeling and analysis of trust management for cognitive mission-driven group communication systems in mobile ad hoc networks. In: International Conference on Computational Science and Engineering; IEEE; 2009. pp. 641–650.

[18] Kohlas, R., Jonczy, J. and Haenni, R. A trust evaluation method based on logic and probability theory. In: IFIP International Conference on Trust Management; Springer US; 2008. pp. 17–32.

[19] Reidt, S., Wolthusen, S.D. and Balfe, S. Robust and efficient communication overlays for trust authority computations. In: Sarnoff Symposium (SARNOFF); IEEE; 2009. pp. 1–5.

[20] Jhaveri, R.H. and Patel, N.M. A sequence number based bait detection scheme to thwart grayhole attack in mobile ad hoc networks. Wireless Networks. 2015;**21**(8):2781–2798.

[21] Jhaveri, R.H. and Patel, N.M. Evaluating energy efficiency of secure routing schemes for mobile ad-hoc networks. International Journal of Next-Generation Computing. 2016;**7**(2):130–143.

Chapter 3

Performance Analysis of Three Routing Protocols in MANET Using the NS-2 and ANOVA Test with Varying Speed of Nodes

Subhrananda Goswami, Subhankar Joardar,
Chandan Bikash Das, Samarajit Kar and
Dibyendu Kumar Pal

Additional information is available at the end of the chapter

http://dx.doi.org/10.5772/66521

Abstract

In this chapter, we analyzed ad hoc on demand distance vector (AODV), dynamic source routing (DSR), and destination-sequenced distance vector (DSDV) routing protocols using different parameters of QoS metrics such as packet delivery ratio (PDR), normalize routing overhead, throughput, and jitter. The aim of this chapter is to determine a difference between routing protocol performance when operating in a large-area MANET with high-speed mobile nodes. After the simulations, we use AWK to analyze the data and then Xgraph to plot the performance metric. After that we use one-way ANOVA tools to confirm the correctness of the result. We use NS-2 for the simulation work. The comparison analysis of these protocols will be carrying out and in the last, we conclude that which routing protocol is the best one for mobile ad hoc networks.

Keywords: AODV, DSR, DSDV, MANET, throughput, packet delivery ratio, jitter, NS-2, ANOVA

1. Introduction

The existing literature on MANETs is very extensive. An extremely comprehensive work is presented in Refs. [1, 2], which extensively covers most issues related to the subject, whereas in Refs. [3, 4], authors provide a brief introduction. MANET design issues such as a routing architecture in the light of the nature of MANETS, unidirectional link support, QoS routing, and multicast support are discussed in Refs. [5, 6]. In Ref. [7], the authors cover some of the same design issues as mentioned in Ref. [5], but they augment them with some additional ones, such as limited bandwidth, energy constrained operation, and limited physical security.

Communication networks are evolving with a great pace witnessing increase in infrastructure and applications too. A mobile ad hoc network is the latest outcome in this research. The mobile ad hoc network, also known as MANET [8], is a network without any available infrastructure.

Nodes are mobile and can move whenever and wherever they want, because there is no centralized control or any other infrastructure is needed in any MANET. Each node in an MANET must be capable of functioning as a router to relay the traffic of other nodes.

A number of protocols have been developed for accomplish this task. Various dedicated routing protocols have been proposed to the Internet Engineering Task Force (IETF) MANET Working Group [8]. Some of these protocols have been studied, and their performances have been analyzed in detail. Broch et al. [9] evaluated four protocols using mobility and traffic scenarios similar to those we used. They focused on packet loss, routing message overhead, and route length. In Ref. [10], Johansson et al. compare three routing protocols, over extensive scenarios, varying node mobility, and traffic load. They focus on packet loss, routing overhead, throughput, and delay, and introduce mobility measures in terms of node relative speed. Finally, in Ref. [11], Das and coworkers compare the performance of two protocols, focusing on packet loss, packet end-to-end delay, and routing load. They obtained simulation results consistent with previous works and conclude with some recommendations for improving protocols. In this chapter, we measure and compare three performance parameter behaviors of two routing protocols, respectively, ad hoc on demand distance vector (AODV) [12] and destination-sequenced distance vector (DSDV).

2. MANET routing protocols

This is the leading routing protocol proposed so for in the category of on demand or reactive routing protocols. Unlike table-driven protocols, it does not maintain status of the network via continuous updates [13]. This approach assists in minimizing the flooded messages and also size of route tables. It was designed after a distance vector routing protocol (DSDV) but is much efficient than DSDV. Actually, AODV is a combination of DSDV and dynamic source routing (DSR). It has the actual on-demand technique of discovering the route and also route maintenance from DSR but uses sequence numbering and also the periodic beacons of DSDV. New routes are found through the process of RREQ and RREP where RREQ packets are broadcast and RREPs are unicast in nature. While route maintenance uses RERR packets for remedy of route breaks, routing information is kept afresh by the usage of sequence numbers, which is the idea borrowed from DSDV [14].

The DSDV [15] is a proactive routing algorithm based upon a well-known classical distance vector algorithm of Bellman-Ford. Routing tables are maintained and updated accordingly, so broadcast periodic routing table update packets consume the bandwidth. So, the main weakness of DSDV is that when network grows these packets also increase. The main improvement here to the Bellman-Ford algorithm is loop freedom, which is made possible by assigning the sequence number to each entry in the routing table, which avoids stale routes.

The dynamic source routing (DSR) [10] is an on-demand or reactive routing protocol. Therefore, unlike other proactive routing protocols, DSR involves no updates of whichever type at any stage inside the network. The DSR uses source routing for forwarding data packets, which distinguishes DSR from other reactive routing protocols. It is lightweight on inner routers due to source routing, the maintaining routing information is not needed at every host. The sender becomes aware of complete destination address before transmission and appends this address in the header of the routing data packet at the beginning. It is loop free due to source routing. Extensive use of cache and promiscuously listening are the main optimizations to DSR when network is at low mobility.

3. Simulation model

The simulation software used in this chapter is the network simulator, NS-2 [16, 17]. The software version used is the latest release at the time of the commencement of simulation, namely, ns-2.34, which can be downloaded from Ref. [17]. In addition, many existing ad hoc routing protocol modules have already been implemented in NS-2. Three such protocols are AODV, DSR, and DSDV. NS-2 is a discrete-event-driven simulation software targeted for network simulation. This software is currently maintained by the Information Science Institute of University of Southern California.

3.1. Simulation evaluation methodology

In order to analyze and compare the performance of the three routing protocols AODV, DSR, and DSDV, simulation experiments were performed. The purpose of the simulations was to compare the efficiency of the routing protocols based on different simulation parameters. The focus was concentrated on four performance metrics:

(1) Packet delivery ratio (PDR).

(2) Throughput.

(3) Normalized routing overhead.

(4) Jitter.

3.2. Results

Generated trace file that is (.tr)

r -t 2.046566484 -Hs 1 -Hd -1 -Ni 1 -Nx 454.33 -Ny 337.37 -Nz 0.00 -Ne 9.996194 -Nl RTR -Nw — -Ma 0 -Md ffffffff -Ms 4 -Mt 800 -Is 1.255 -Id 9.255 -It DSR -Il 48 -If 0 -Ii 17 -Iv 32 -P dsr -Ph 2 -Pq 1 -Ps 2 -Pp 0 -Pn 2 -Pl 0 -Pe 0->16 -Pw 0 -Pm 0 -Pc 0 -Pb 0->0

3.3. NAM file output

NAM is a Tcl/TK-based animation tool for viewing network simulation traces and real-world packet traces. Taking data from network simulators (such as ns) or live networks, NAM was one of the first tools to provide general purpose, packet-level, and network animation, before starting to use NAM, a trace file needs to create [16]. This trace file is usually generated by NS. Once the trace file is generated, NAM can be used to animate it. A snapshot of the simulation topology in NAM for 15 mobile nodes is shown in **Figure 1**, which is visualized the traces of communication or packet movements between mobile nodes [17].

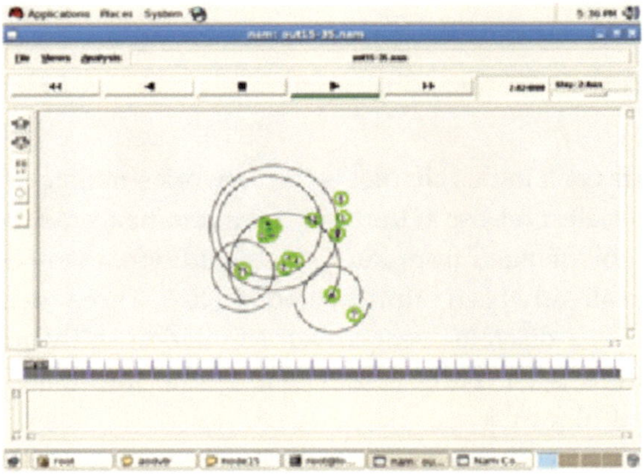

Figure 1. A simple NAM file output.

The NAM file output for packet dropping is shown in **Figure 2**.

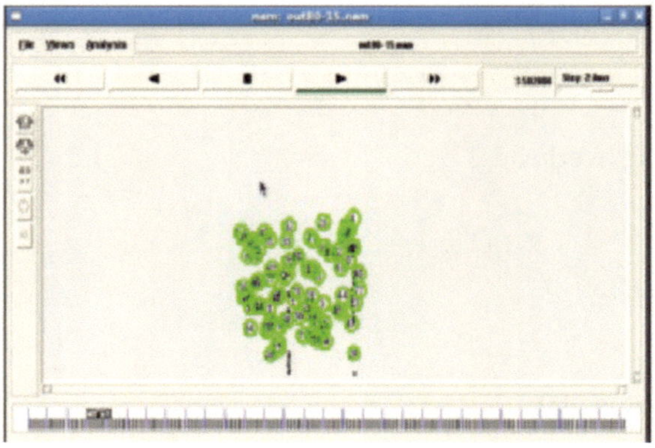

Figure 2. A NAM output with packet dropping.

4. Simulation results and observation

4.1. Packet delivery ratio (PDR)

Packet delivery ratio (PDR) is defined as the ratio of data packets delivered successfully to destination nodes and the total number of data packets generated for those destinations. PDR characterizes the packet loss rate, which limits the throughput of the network. The higher the delivery ratio, better the performance of the routing protocol. The ratio of the data delivered to the destination to the data sent out by the source. PDR is determined as

$$PDR = \left(\frac{\text{Received packets}}{\text{Sent packets}}\right) * 100 \quad (1)$$

Figures 3–6 clearly indicate that the AODV routing protocol outcomes are better with the CBR traffic. AODV protocol performs better in comparison of other two selected routing protocols in such a network environment with varying speeds of nodes. So, we conclude that AODV is better in most of the PDR cases.

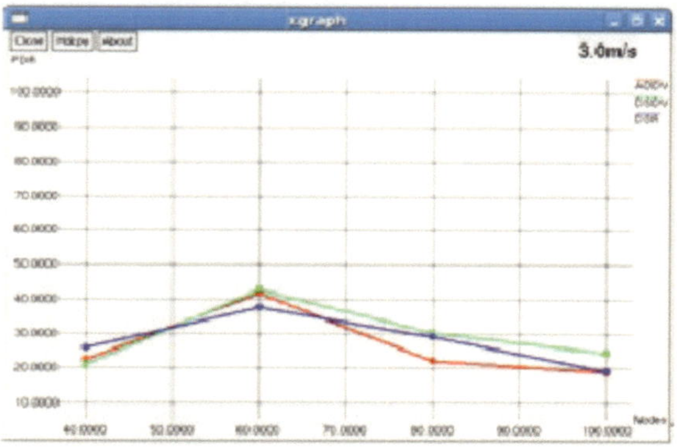

Figure 3. Packet delivery ratio (PDR) at 3 m/s.

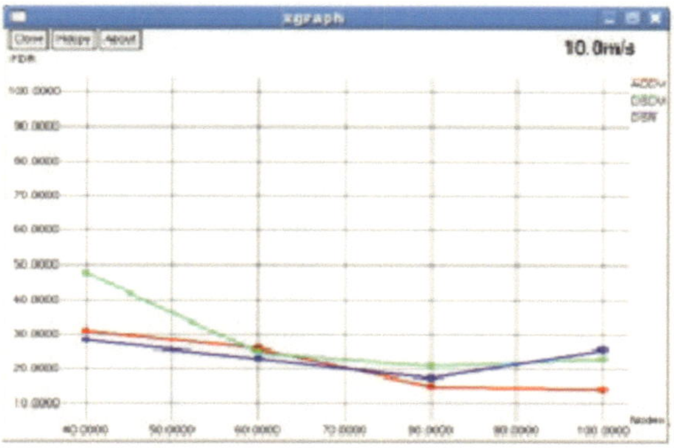

Figure 4. Packet delivery ratio (PDR) at 10 m/s.

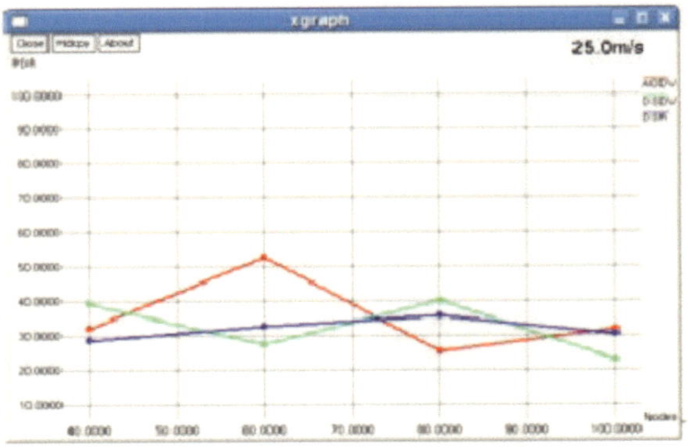

Figure 5. Packet delivery ratio (PDR) at 25 m/s.

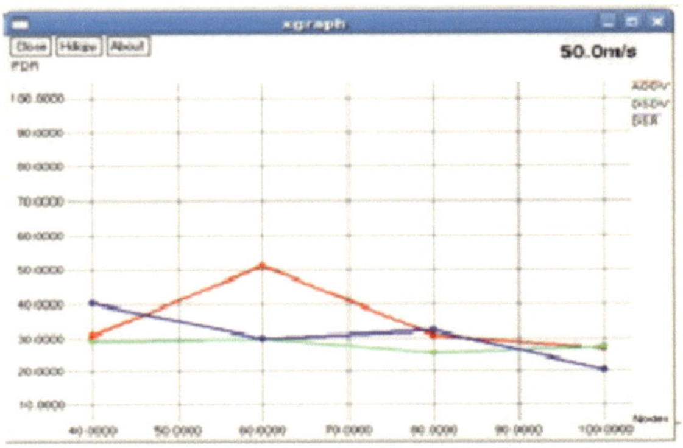

Figure 6. Packet delivery ratio (PDR) at 50 m/s.

4.2. Throughput

Throughput is defined as the ratio of the total data reaches a receiver from the sender. The time it takes by the receiver to receive the last message is called as throughput. Throughput is expressed as bytes or bits per sec (byte/sec or bit/sec). Some factors affect the throughput as; if there are many topology changes in the network, unreliable communication between nodes, limited bandwidth available, and limited energy. A high throughput is absolute choice in every network. Throughput can be represented mathematically as in equation. This represents the number of packets received by the destination within a given time interval. It is a measure of effectiveness of a routing protocol.

$$\text{Throughput} = \frac{\text{File size}}{\text{Transmission time (bps)}} \tag{2}$$

$$\text{Transmission time (bps)} = \frac{\text{File size}}{\text{Bandwidth (sec)}} \tag{3}$$

The analysis of **Figures 7–10** shows that performance of AODV is better than DSR and DSDV. Another characteristic that has come to the notice is that pause time does not have significant bearing on the throughput, whereas the performance is dictated only by the density of the network.

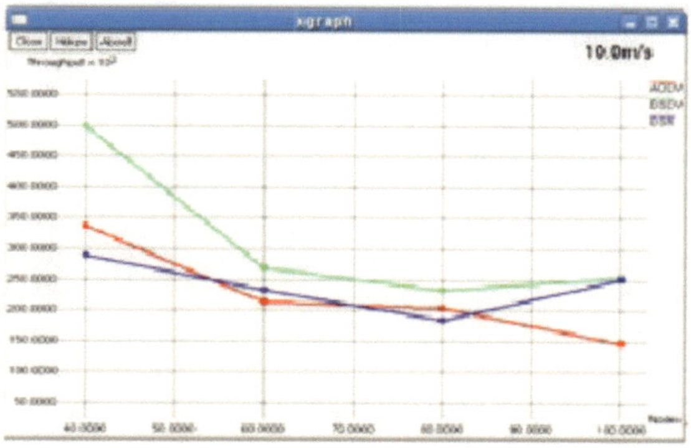

Figure 7. Throughput at 3 m/s.

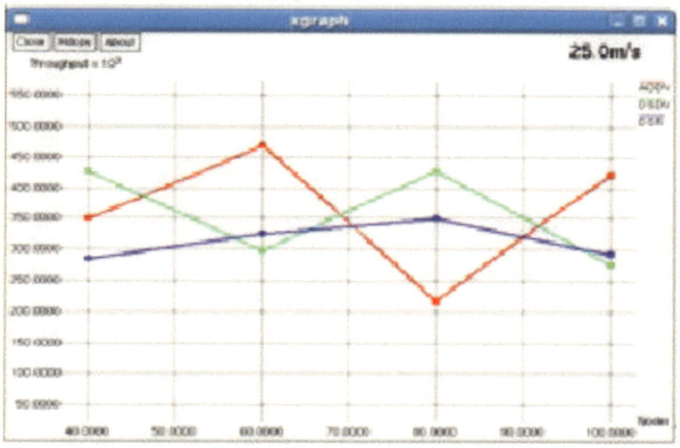

Figure 8. Throughput at 10 m/s.

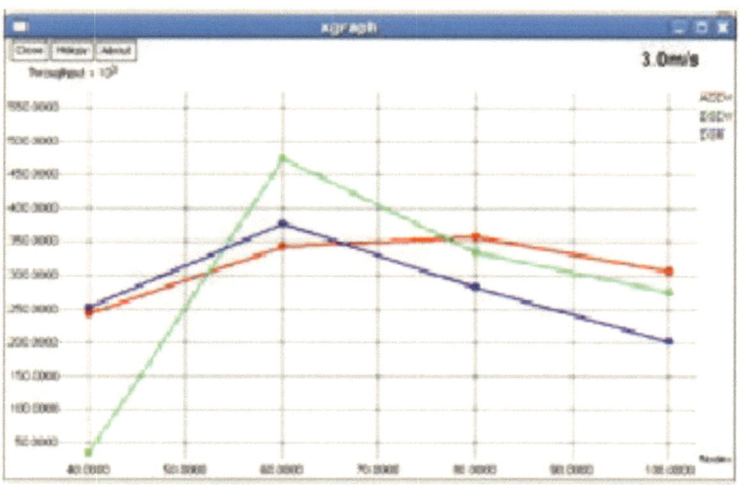

Figure 9. Throughput at 25 m/s.

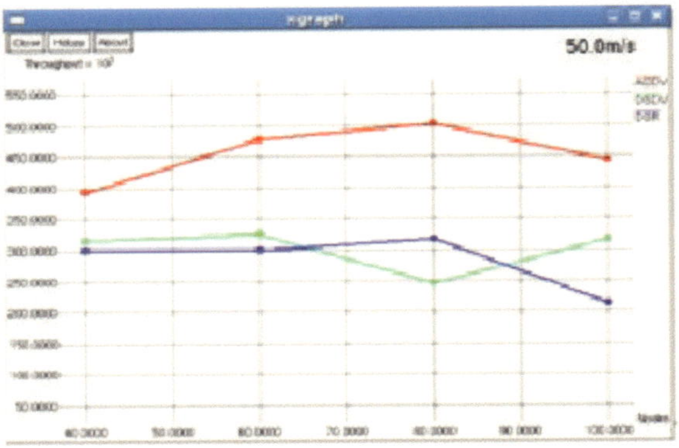

Figure 10. Throughput at 50 m/s.

4.3. Normalized routing overhead

This is the ratio of routing-related transmissions (RREQ, RREP, RERR, etc.) to data transmissions in a simulation. A transmission is one node either sending or forwarding a packet. Either way, the routing load per unit data successfully delivered to the destination.

It is the total number of control or routing (RTR) packets generated by routing protocol during the simulation. All packets sent or forwarded at network layer is consider routing overhead.

$$\text{Routing overhead} = \text{Number of RTR packets} \tag{4}$$

Based on the result of simulation, **Figures 11–14** show that the performance of DSDV is better than AODV and DSR. At all the considered mobility, DSDV is the best protocol as compared to other protocols.

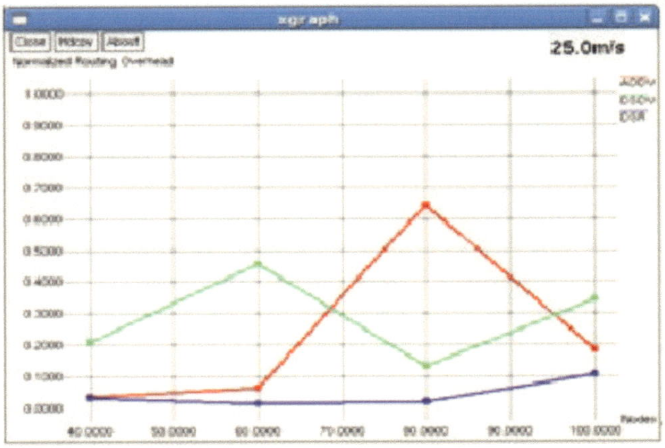

Figure 11. Normalized routing overhead at 3 m/s.

http://dx.doi.org/10.5772/66521

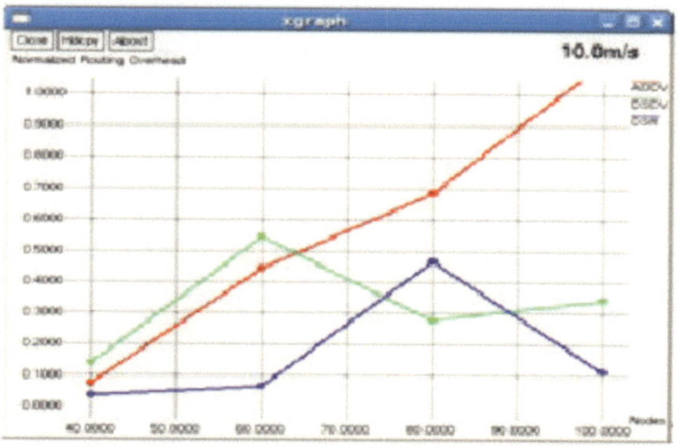

Figure 12. Normalized routing overhead at 10 m/s.

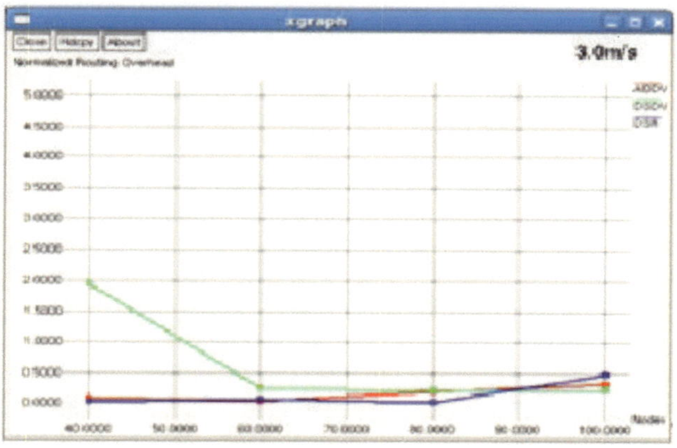

Figure 13. Normalized routing overhead at 25 m/s.

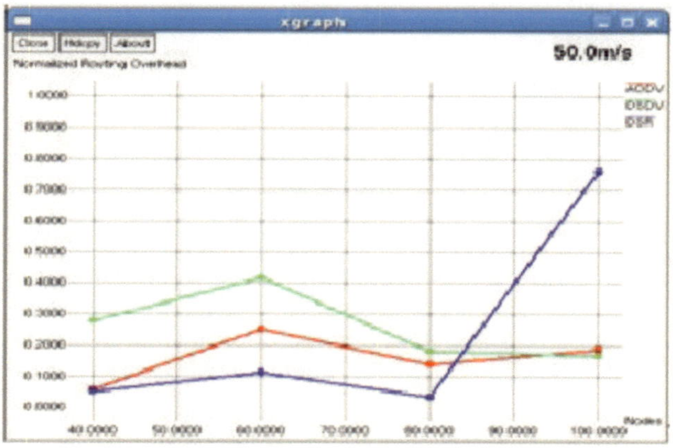

Figure 14. Normalized routing overhead at 50 m/s.

4.4. Jitter

The term jitter is often used as a measure of the variability over time of the packet latency across a network. A network with constant latency has no variation (or jitter). Packet jitter is expressed as an average of the deviation from the network mean latency. However, for this use, the term is imprecise [13]. Or in other words, jitter is the variation of the packet arrival time. In jitter calculation, the variation in the packet arrival time is expected to minimum. The delays between the different packets need to be low if we want better performance in mobile ad hoc networks.

Based on the result of simulation, **Figures 15** and **16** show that the performance of AODV and DSR gives the better result. **Figures 17** and **18** show that DSR gives the better performance.

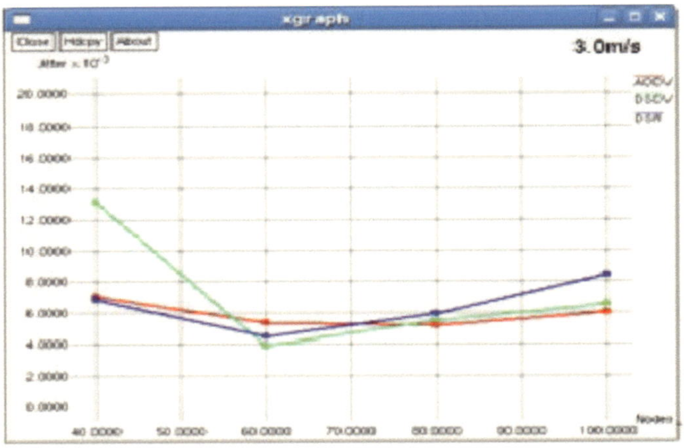

Figure 15. Jitter at 3 m/s.

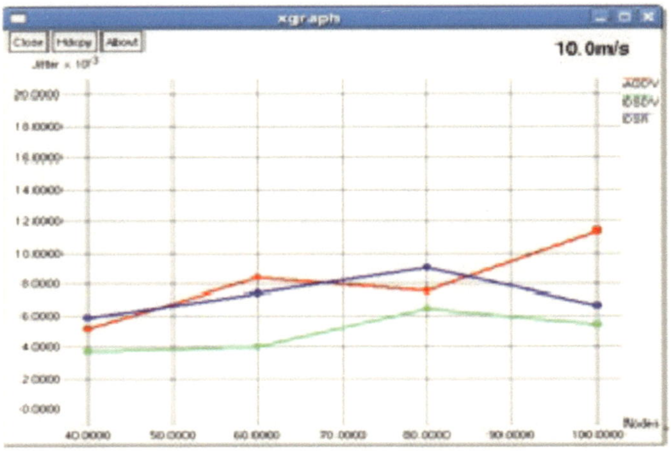

Figure 16. Jitter at 10 m/s.

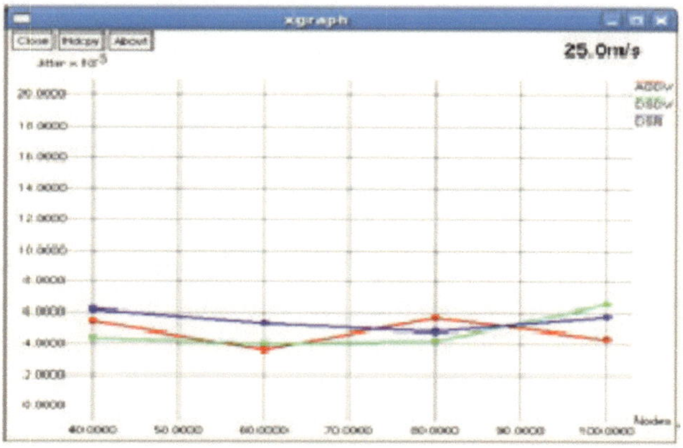

Figure 17. Jitter at 25 m/s.

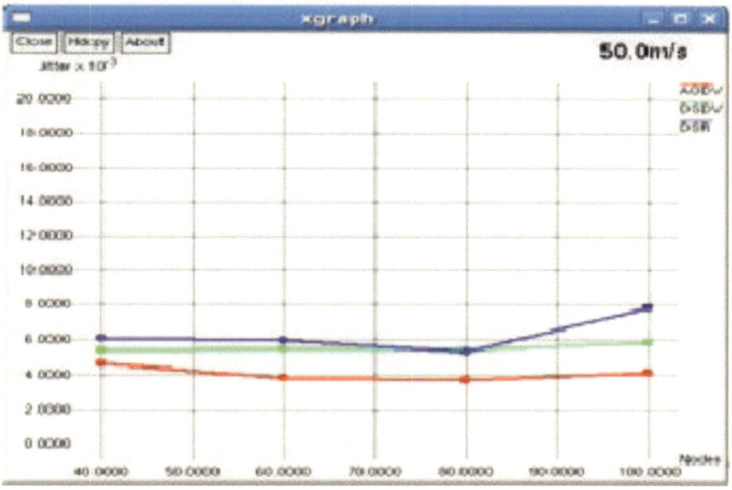

Figure 18. Jitter at 50 m/s.

5. ANOVA test

Analysis of variance (ANOVA) is a collection of statistical models used to analyze the differences between group means and their associated procedures (such as "variation" among and between groups), in which the observed variance in a particular variable is partitioned into components attributable to different sources of variation [18].

In this chapter, we have use one-way ANOVA. One-way ANOVA is used to study the effect of ($k > 2$) levels of a single factor. A factor is defined as characteristics under consideration, thought to influence the measured observation. A level is defined as a value of a factor.

5.1. Output of the test for different parameters

5.1.1. Packet delivery ratio

The packet delivery ratio (PDR) is very much related to the throughput metric. The destination records the number of data packets it received and estimates the PDR delivery ratio in the network from the count of the data packets sent. The ANOVA hypothesis test is shown in **Table 1**, there is sufficient evidence to reject the null hypothesis. We see that there is a significant different in PDR performance when the network adopts different routing methods (P-value > 0.05).

Groups	Count	Sum	Average	Variance
AODV	23	802.8693	34.90736	121.3164733
DSDV	23	744.1666	32.35507	171.2711624
DSR	23	729.8366	31.73203	56.06334723

Table 1. Summary of packet delivery ratio.

The one-way ANOVA test for PDR is shown in **Table 2**.

In this case, F_{crit} = 3.135918 at α = 0.05. Since F = 0.560241875 < 3.135918, the results are significant at the 5% significance level. So, we will accept the null hypothesis, and conclusion can be drawn that there is strong evidence that the expected values in the three groups do not differ. The variation is quite small and can be eliminated at this significance level. The P-value for this test is 0.573763.

Source of variation	SS	Df	MS	F	P-value	F_{crit}
Between groups	130.21925	2	65.10963	0.560241875	0.573763	3.135918
Within groups	7670.3216	66	116.217			
Total	7800.5409	68				

Table 2. ANOVA of packet delivery ratio.

5.1.2. Throughput

Data throughput is defined as the total number of packets delivered over the total simulation time. ANOVA statistical computation shows that we do not reject the null hypothesis. That is, there is no significant difference for the different methods in terms of throughput performance (P-value > 0.05) (**Table 3**).

http://dx.doi.org/10.5772/66521

Groups	Count	Sum	Average	Variance
AODV	23	7990941	347432.2	8201779957
DSDV	23	8094695	351943.3	20237752574
DSR	23	7267943	315997.5	5554377965

Table 3. Summary of throughput.

The one-way ANOVA test for throughput is shown in **Table 4**.

Source of variation	SS	df	MS	F	P-value	F_{crit}
Between groups	1.764E+10	2	8.82E+09	0.778278814	0.463364	3.135918
Within groups	7.479E+11	66	1.13E+10			
Total	7.655E+11	68				

Table 4. ANOVA of throughput.

In this case, F_{crit} = 3.135918 at α = 0.05. Since F = 0.778278814 < 3.135918, the results are significant at the 5% significance level. So, we will accept the null hypothesis, and conclusion can be drawn that there is strong evidence that the expected values in the three groups do not differ. The variation is quite small and can be eliminated at this significance level. The P-value for this test is 0.463364.

5.1.3. Normalized routing overhead

Using the ANOVA hypothesis testing, the simulation results show a significant difference among methods used in terms of normalized routing overhead (P-value > 0.05). Thus, normalized routing overhead can be used as a metric to measure the performance of different algorithms (**Table 5**).

Groups	Count	Sum	Average	Variance
AODV	23	2.19207	0.095307	0.01199388
DSDV	23	13.66286	0.594037	0.846600923
DSR	23	0.528887	0.022995	0.000264522

Table 5. Summary of normalized routing overhead.

The one-way ANOVA test for normalized routing overhead is shown in **Table 6**.

Source of variation	SS	df	MS	F	P-value	F_{crit}
Between groups	4.4470485	2	2.223524	7.766781596	0.000935	3.135918
Within groups	18.894905	66	0.286286			
Total	23.341954	68				

Table 6. ANOVA of normalized routing overhead.

In this case, $F_{crit} = 3.135918$ at $\alpha = 0.05$. Since $F = 7.766781596 > 3.135918$, the results are significant at the 5% significance level. So, we will reject the null hypothesis, and conclusion can be drawn that there is strong evidence that the expected values in the three groups differ significantly. The P-value for this test is 0.000935.

5.1.4. *Jitter*

The term jitter often used as a measure of the packet of the variability over time of the packet latency across a network. A network with constant latency has no variation (or jitter). Packet jitter is expressed as an average of the derivation from the network mean latency. ANOVA statistical computation shows that we do not reject the null hypothesis. That is, there is no significant difference for the different methods in terms of throughput performance (P-value > 0.05) (**Table 7**).

Groups	Count	Sum	Average	Variance
AODV	23	0.129171	0.005616	2.07E−06
DSDV	23	0.125752	0.005467	5.9E−06
DSR	23	0.131442	0.005715	1.91E−06

Table 7. Summary of jitter.

The one-way ANOVA test for jitter is shown in **Table 8**.

Source of variation	SS	df	MS	F	P-value	F_{crit}
Between Groups	7.14E−07	2	3.57E−07	0.108241	0.89757	3.135918
Within Groups	0.000218	66	3.3E−06			
Total	0.000218	68				

Table 8. ANOVA of jitter.

In this case, $F_{crit} = 3.135918$ at $\alpha = 0.05$. Since $F = 0.108241 < 3.135918$, the results are significant at the 5% significance level. So, we will accept the null hypothesis, and conclusion can be drawn that

http://dx.doi.org/10.5772/66521

there is strong evidence that the expected values in the three groups do not differ. The variation is quite small and can be eliminated at this significance level. The *P*-value for this test is 0.89757.

6. Conclusion

The results indicate that the performance is better especially when the number of nodes in the network is higher. In this chapter, we have used a simulator that provides the virtual environment for the testing different parameters. Reactive routing protocol AODV performance is the best considering due to its ability to maintain connection by periodic exchange of information. Using NS-2 simulator we created the scenarios under which using tcl script, it is run. After analyzing the X-graphs, we concluded that AODV indicates its highest efficiency and performance under high mobility than DSR and DSDV, and the performance of TCP and UDP packets with respect to normalized routing overhead, jitter, throughput, and PDR, and the performance of AODV is better than DSDV and DSR routing protocol for real-time applications from the simulation results.

After that in one-way ANOVA test, AODV exhibits better routing performance compared with conventional routing methods such as DSDV and DSR. By performing an ANOVA analysis at the initial stage, we conclude that there is a significant difference in the performance metrics when using different routing algorithms. From there, we analyze the difference of the means and boundaries in 95% confidence interval. In all simulation scenarios, we see that AODV shows a lower packet loss and lower delay. It offers higher throughput and ensures higher packet delivery ratio.

Author details

Subhrananda Goswami[1,*], Subhankar Joardar[2], Chandan Bikash Das[3], Samarajit Kar[4] and Dibyendu Kumar Pal[5]

*Address all correspondence to: subhrananda_usca@yahoo.co.in

1 Department of Information Technology, Global Group of Institutions, Haldia, Purba Midnapore, West Bengal, India

2 Department of CSE, Haldia Institute of Technology, Haldia, Purba Medinipur, West Bengal, India

3 Department of Mathematics, Tamralipta Mahavidyalaya, Tamluk, Purba Midnapore, West Bengal, India

4 Department of Mathematics, National Institute of Technology, Durgapur, Burdwan, West Bengal, India

5 Department Of Computer Application, Asansol Engineering College, Asansol, Burdwan, West Bengal, India

References

[1] Murthy R.S.C. and Manoj B.S. Ad Hoc Wireless Networks- Architectures. Prentice Hall, Upper Saddle River, NJ, 2004.

[2] Goswami S., Joardar S., Das C.B., and Das B. A simulation based performance comparison of AODV and DSDV mobile ad hoc networks. Information Technology and Computer Science. 2014;**6**(10):11–18.

[3] Remondo D. Tutorial on wireless ad hoc networks [Internet]. 2004. Available from: www.comp.brad.ac.uk/het-net/HET-NETs04/CameraPapers/T2.pdf

[4] Goswami S., Joardar S., and Das C.B. Performance Comparison of Routing Protocols of MANET Using NS-2. 1st ed. Germany: LAP LAMBERT Academic Publishing; 2014, 141p.

[5] Chun Y.L. and Lin S.M. Routing protocols overview and design issues for self-organized-network [sic]. International Conference on Communication Technology Proceedings; Beijing, China. 2000, pp. 1298–1303.

[6] Goswami S., Joardar S., and Das C.B. Reactive and proactive routing protocol performance metric comparison in mobile ad hoc networks using NS 2. International Journal of Advanced Research in Computer and Communication Engineering. 2014;**3**(1):4908–4914.

[7] Macker J.P. and Corson M.S. Mobile ad hoc networking (MANET):Routing protocol performance issues and evaluation considerations (Internet-draft), in: *Mobile Ad-hoc Network (MANET) Working Group, IETF*. 1998.

[8] Internet Engineering Task Force MANET Working Group Charter. Available from: www.ietf,org/html.charters/manet-charter.html; 1999

[9] Broch J., Maltz D.A., Johnson D.B., Hu Y.C., and Jetcheva J. A performance comparisonof multi-hop wireless ad hoc network routing protocols. Proceedings of the Fourth Annual ACM; IEEE International Conference on Mobile Computing and Networking; 1998, pp. 85–97.

[10] Broch J., Maltz D.A., and Johnson D.B. The dynamic source routing protocol for mobilead hoc networks. Internet Draft, MANET Working Group. 1999.

[11] Perkins C.E., Royer E.M., and Das S.R. Performance comparison of two on-demand routing protocols for ad hoc networks. in *IEEE Personal Communications*. vol. 8. no. 1. pp. 16–28. 2001.

[12] Perkins C.E. and Royer E.M. Ad hoc on-demand distance vector (AODV) routing. Internet Draft, MANET Working Group. 2000.

[13] Belding-Royer E.M., Perkins C.E., and Chakeres I. *Ad hoc On-Demand Distance Vector (AODV) Routing: Work in progress*. July 2004. Internet Draft, RFC 3561bis-01, http:// moment. cs. ucsb. edu/pub/draft-perkins-manet-aodvbis-02. txt.

[14] Papadimitratos P. and Haas Z.J. Secure on-demand distance vector routing in ad hoc networks. *IEEE/Sarnoff Symposium on Advances in Wired and Wireless Communication.* Princeton, NJ, 2005, pp. 168–171.

[15] Gorantala K. Routing protocols in mobile ad hoc networks [thesis]. Sweden: Umea University; 2006.

[16] nsnam web pages. Network simulator-ns-2 [Internet]. Available from: www.isi.edu/nsnam; 1989.

[17] NS Manual/Documentation-The VINT Project Collaboration between researchers at UC Berkeley, LBL, USC/ISI and Xerox. PARC.KevinFall_kfall@ee.lbl.gov, Kennan Varadhan_kannan@catarina.usc.edu, 1996.

[18] Barman S., Ghosh A., and Biswas S. A transparent tree root identification scheme to support route-optimization and network mobility in PMIPv6 Domain. *IEEE 2nd International Conference on Recent Trends in Information Systems (ReTIS),* Kolkata. 2015. pp. 532–537.

Chapter 4

Cooperative Routing in Multi-Radio Multi-Hop Wireless Network

Kun Xie, Shiming He, Xin Wang, Dafang Zhang and Keqin Li

Additional information is available at the end of the chapter

http://dx.doi.org/10.5772/66414

Abstract

There are many recent interests on cooperative communication (CC) in wireless networks. Despite the large capacity gain of CC in small wireless networks, CC can result in severe interference in large networks and even degraded throughput. The aim of this chapter is to concurrently exploit multi-radio and multi-channel (MRMC) and CC technique to combat co-channel interference and improve the performance of multi-hop wireless network. Our proposed solution concurrently considers cooperative routing, channel assignment, and relay selection and takes advantage of both MRMC technique and spatial diversity to improve the throughput. We propose two important metrics, contention-aware channel utilization routing metric (CACU) to capture the interference cost from both direct and cooperative transmission, and traffic aware channel condition metric (TACC) to evaluate the channel load condition. Based on these metrics, we propose three algorithms for interference-aware cooperative routing, local channel adjustment, and local path and relay adaptation, respectively, to ensure high-performance communications in dynamic wireless networks. Our algorithms are fully distributed and can effectively mitigate co-channel interference and achieve cooperative diversity gain. To our best knowledge, this is the first distributed solution that supports CC in MRMC networks. Our performance studies demonstrate that our algorithms can significantly increase the aggregate throughput.

Keywords: cooperative routing, relay assignment, channel assignment

1. Introduction

As an emerging technique for future wireless networks, cooperative communication (CC) has been proposed to take advantage of the broadcast nature of wireless communications and spatial diversity to improve the network performance [1, 2]. More specifically, relay nodes have been exploited to forward the replica of packets from the sources, and the destinations can combine multiple copies of the signal to better decode the original message. Taking advantage of spatial and multiuser diversities, CC can efficiently improve the network performance.

Despite the significant performance gain in small networks, recent research results show through both analysis and simulation that the use of cooperative relays (CRs) in large-scale wireless networks can lead to severe interference, which in turn results in higher packet loss and consequent throughput reduction [3–5]. Although relay nodes may help to increase the throughput of a single source and destination pair, a cooperative transmission (CT) often involves three transmission links (i.e., from the source to the relay, from the source to the destination, and from the relay to the destination). The increase of transmission links in a neighborhood leads to higher interference, thus reducing the network-wise performance [6]. When the interference is severe, the performance can be even worse than without using cooperative transmissions. It is critical to reduce the interference for CC to work efficiently in a practical wireless network, especially when the network scale is large.

Another recent technique, multi-radio multi-channel (MRMC), has been exploited to alleviate the co-channel interference by supporting concurrent transmissions over orthogonal channels to improve the network capacity [7–9]. With the growth of modern wireless technologies, the cost of radio chips including those supporting 802.11 [10, 11] constantly reduces and more devices will be equipped with multiple radios.

In this chapter, we exploit MRMC to alleviate the interference in a network with cooperative communications for potentially much higher network performance. In cooperative networks, a routing path can be formed with a combination of cooperative transmissions and direct transmissions (DTs), and we call this kind of routing **cooperative routing**. The important and interesting question this chapter tries to answer is what is the maximum aggregate throughput of a multi-radio multi-channel network when the cooperative transmission is available? Current studies on cooperative communications in multi-hop wireless network generally assume that the network nodes are equipped with only a single antenna [12–20], and it is unclear what capacity and performance gain can be achieved if nodes are equipped with multiple antennas. Despite the large potential benefit, it is highly non-trivial to make both CC and MRMC techniques to work seamlessly together. Some of the challenges are as follows.

First, the coupled cooperative routing problem and relay selection problem should be solved together. Different from conventional routing in MRMC networks where every node just needs to find the next-hop node to forward packets toward the destination, with cooperative routing, a neighbor of the transmitter not only needs to serve as a multi-hop transmission relay (MR) for packet forwarding but may also act as a cooperative relay (CR) of the transmitter for cooperative transmission. The capability for a node or a radio interface to serve as two different types of relay makes multi-radio cooperative routing and relay node assignment inter-dependent.

http://dx.doi.org/10.5772/66414

Second, there is a trade-off between alleviating co-channel interference and exploiting cooperative diversity. In single-radio single-channel cooperative wireless networks, one-hop neighbors of a transmitter are candidate MR or CR nodes. A transmitter node can determine to use direct transmission and find an MR or cooperative transmission and find a CR to maximize the cooperative transmission gain. Although MRMC can largely relieve the co-channel interference, only the node, which tunes to the same channel as that of the transmitter, can act as an MR or a CR, which reduces the number of candidate relay nodes. This makes it important and challenging to consider radio-channel assignment along with cooperative communications.

Third, the use of cooperative relays in cooperative communications makes the network interference condition more complicated than that in a network with only direct transmissions, and it desires careful design to reduce the interference along with the finding of the cooperative routing path and channel assignment in MRMC cooperative networks.

In summary, there is an inter-dependence among cooperative routing, channel assignment, and relay selection. To enable cooperative communications in MRMC wireless networks and fulfill the complete potential of both techniques, the three problems need to be systematically solved together. A few recent studies [21–25] have begun to investigate interference-aware cooperative routing algorithms to solve the challenge problems. This chapter presents a practical and distributed solution to effectively exploit both MRMC technique and cooperative diversity to ensure higher performance of a multi-hop network with dynamic channel conditions and traffic flows. In this design, the cooperative routing at the network layer, channel assignment at the MAC layer, and cooperative communication at the physical layer will work interactively and seamlessly together. The main techniques are as follows:

1. Contention-aware channel utilization metric (CACU): this captures the interference cost from both direct transmission and cooperative transmission. Using CACU as the key routing metric, an interference-aware cooperative routing algorithm is proposed.

2. Traffic-aware channel condition metric (TACC): it evaluates the channel load condition and triggers the channel-adjustment procedure to relieve co-channel interference. Based on TACC, a feasible channel selection algorithm is proposed to ensure active flows (involving either direct transmission or cooperative transmission) to have continuous data transmissions during the channel-adjustment process. To further prevent the network from being instable due to channel adjustment, a chain-puzzle detection sub-algorithm is proposed.

3. Local path and relay adjustment algorithm: it further enhances the performance of active flows after channel adjustment.

The remaining of this chapter is organized as follows. We introduce our system model in Section 2. Motivation example and solution overview are presented in Section 3. We present the detailed algorithms on cooperative routing, channel assignment, and local path and relay adjustment in Sections 4–6, respectively. The complete solution is presented in Section 7. Simulation results are given in Section 8. We conclude the work in Section 9.

2. System model

We consider a multi-hop cooperative wireless network where a node can be equipped with multiple radios. We call this network MRMC cooperative wireless network. There are N nodes in the network. Each node i in the network is equipped with one or more radio interfaces (wireless NIC), represented by $I(i)$. Each radio can serve as a transmitter or a receiver on a channel at a given time. We assume that there are a total of K orthogonal channels in the network, numbered $Ch_1, Ch_2, \ldots, Ch_K$, and there is no inter-channel interference. The channel assignment is trivial if the number of orthogonal channels available is at most the minimum number of radios per node $I(i)$, since in this case every node must be assigned all the channels. This chapter assumes that K is larger than $\max_{i \in N} I(i)$. A radio is capable of selecting a working channel from the set of orthogonal channels, and the set of working channels of node i is denoted as $w(i)$. Due to the interference constraints, there is no capacity benefit in equipping two different radios of a node with the same channel. There are multiple concurrent flows, denoted by a set $F = \{F_1, F_2, \ldots, F_M\}$ of M flows. The data for each flow may traverse multiple hops in the network. A flow $F_i(S_i \to D_i)$ goes through a pair of source node and destination node, denoted as S_i and D_i, respectively.

There are two transmission modes between any two nodes in the network considered, direct transmission (DT) and cooperative transmission (CT), as shown in **Figure 1**. Direct transmission mode is widely employed in current wireless networks, where a source node transmits its signal directly to a destination node. The achievable rate of $C_{DT}(S, D)$ between S and D is expressed as follows:

$$C_{DT}(S, D) = W * \log_2(1 + SNR(S, D)). \quad (1)$$

A cooperative transmission involves three nodes and three links. Specifically, a collaborative neighbor R overhears the signal from source S and forwards the signal to the destination D, which then combines two signal streams, $S \to D$ and $R \to D$, into a single stream that has a higher resistance to channel fading and noise and hence a higher probability of being successfully decoded. The mechanism to accomplish CT is not unique. In Ref. [3], the authors describe and compare the capacity of different cooperative transmission protocols and show

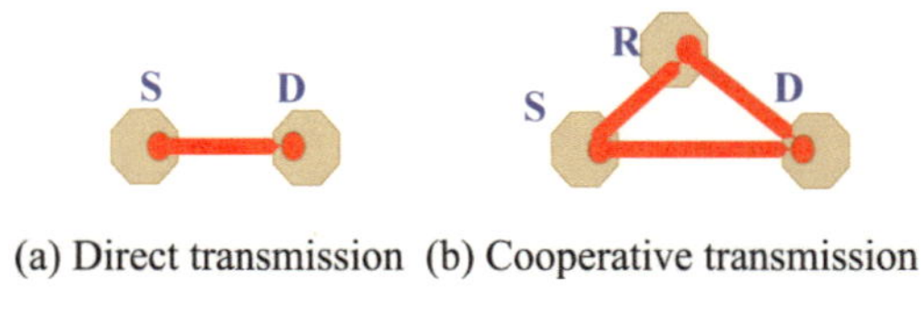

Figure 1. Two kinds of transmission modes.

http://dx.doi.org/10.5772/66414

that the AF-RAKE-based cooperative transmission protocol can achieve the maximum capacity. In AF-RAKE, R receives signals from S and amplifies and forwards them to D without demodulation or decoding. D uses a RAKE receiver to combine both signal streams of $S \rightarrow D$ and $R \rightarrow D$. The achievable rate of $C_{CT}(S, R, D)$ between S and D with R as relay under AF-RAKE mode [3] is given by

$$C_{CT}(S, R, D) = W * \log_2(1 + SNR(S, D) + \frac{SNR(S, R) * SNR(R, D)}{SNR(S, R) + SNR(R, D) + 1}), \tag{2}$$

$$SNR(m, n) = \frac{P_m}{\sigma_n^2} \left| h_{m,n} \right|^2. \tag{3}$$

In the above equation, P_m denotes the transmission power at node m. $h_{m,n}$ captures the effects of path loss, shadowing, and fading within the channel between m and n. The noise components are modeled as white Gaussian noise (AWGN). σ_n^2 denotes variance of the background noise at nodes n.

Relay nodes can be categorized into two types based on their functions: a cooperative relay (CR), which operates at the physical layer for cooperative transmission (i.e., node R_6 in flow F_3 in **Figure 2**), and a multi-hop relay (MR), which operates at the network layer to relay packets from a source over multiple hops to its destination (i.e., node R_1 in flow F_2 in **Figure 2**). A node with multiple radios can serve as both CR and MR for multiple flows. For example, R_3 acts as CR relay in F_3, but MR relay for F_4. More complex function roles can be found on R_7, which acts as CR relay in both F_1 and F_3, and MR relay in F_2.

A cooperative routing path could be a combination of cooperative transmissions and direct transmissions. For example, flow $F_3(S_3 \rightarrow D_3) = S_3 \xrightarrow{Ch_2} R_2(R_3) \xrightarrow{Ch_3} R_4(R_7) \xrightarrow{Ch_1} R_5 \xrightarrow{Ch_2} D_3(R_6)$, in **Figure 2**, where the first hop link $l^{Ch_2}_{S_3R_2(R_3)}$, the second hop link $l^{Ch_3}_{R_2R_4(R_7)}$, and the fourth hop link $l^{Ch_2}_{R_5D_3(R_6)}$ adopt cooperative transmission mode with nodes R_3, R_7, and R_6 acting as CR relays, respectively, while the third hop link $l^{Ch_1}_{R_4R_5}$ adopts the direct transmission mode with both R_4 and R_5 being MR relays.

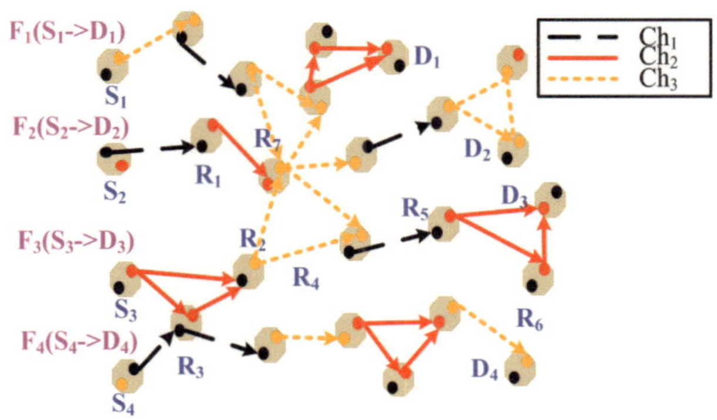

Figure 2. The MRMC cooperative network.

3. Motivation example and solution overview

To help understand the significance of our problem, we first give a motivation example to show that only channel assignment and cooperative routing cannot achieve the good performance. Expired from the example, we give an overview on our solution.

Figure 3 is an MRMC cooperative wireless network consisting of 14 nodes. The small solid dots in each node denote the radios. There are three orthogonal channels available, denoted by Ch_1, Ch_2 and Ch_3. For simplicity, we assume that all the links are free of transmission error, and the raw capacity of each link can be calculated by Eq. (1) or (2) depending on the transmission mode. The communication range and interference range are set to 250 and 550 m, respectively. The network is connected under an initial channel assignment [26] to guarantee the connectivity of network to transmit any possible flows over multiple hops.

Initially, there are two flows with their routing paths $F_1(A \rightarrow K) = A \xrightarrow{Ch_2} F \xrightarrow{Ch_3} K$ and F_2 $(D \rightarrow E) = D \xrightarrow{Ch_1} B \xrightarrow{Ch_3} E$, as shown in **Figure 3a**. According to Eq. (1), the raw capacity of links in these two flows can be calculated directly: $C_{DT}(A,F)$ = 61.189 Mbps, $C_{DT}(F,K)$ = 65.9819 Mbps, $C_{DT}(D,B)$ = 73.1874 Mbps, $C_{DT}(B,E)$ = 78.8452 Mbps. On channel Ch_3, there are two co-channel links that interfere with each other, link $l_{FK}^{Ch_3}$ passed by flow F_1 and link $l_{BE}^{Ch_3}$ passed by flow F_2. A straightforward way to avoid interference is to apply TDMA to fairly allocate time slots to different flows. As a result, the available capacity of these two links becomes $C_{DT}{'}(F,K) = C_{DT}(F,K)/2$ = 32.9909 Mbps, $C_{DT}{'}(B,E) = C_{DT}(B,E)/2$ = 39.4226 Mbps. Assume that all flows transmit a packet at the peak link data rate through a rough calculation that neglects the overhead cost. Constrained by the bottleneck rate of the path, the end-to-end throughput of $Flow_1$ and $Flow_2$ are $\min\{C_{DT}(A,F), C_{DT}{'}(F,K)\}$ = 32.9909 Mbps and $\min\{C_{DT}(D,B), C_{DT}{'}(B,E)\}$ = 39.4226 Mbps. The aggregate network throughput of these two flows is 32.9909 + 39.4226 = 72.4135 Mbps.

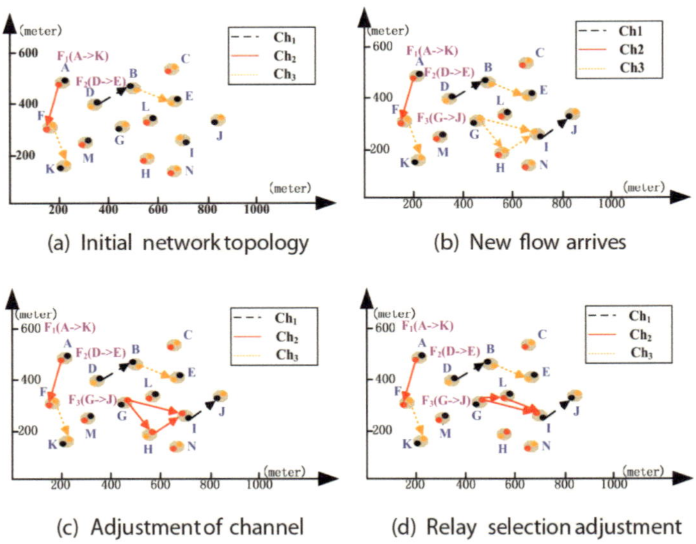

(a) Initial network topology

(b) New flow arrives

(c) Adjustment of channel

(d) Relay selection adjustment

Figure 3. Motivation example.

In **Figure 3b**, a new flow $F_3(G\rightarrow J)$ arrives. To obtain higher cooperative diversity in the network, the potential route for F_3 is chosen as $F_3(G\rightarrow J) = G \xrightarrow{Ch_3} I(H) \xrightarrow{Ch_1} J$, where H acts as the CR relay in the flow path. Similarly, the raw capacity of each hop links $l_{GI(H)}^{Ch_3}$, and $l_{IJ}^{Ch_1}$ can be calculated, with $C_{DT}(I, J) = 91.8365$ Mbps, $C_{CT}(G, H, I) = 51.3242$ Mbps. However, there are two co-channel links that interfere with each other on the channel Ch_1, and three co-channel links on the channel Ch_3, respectively. The available capacity of these links is calculated as follows: $C_{DT}'(A, F) = C_{DT}(A, F) = 61.189$ Mbps, $C_{DT}'(F, K) = C_{DT}(F, K)/3 = 21.90$ Mbps, $C_{DT}'(D, B) = C_{DT}(D, B)/2 = 36.5937$ Mbps, $C_{DT}'(B, E) = C_{DT}(B, E)/3 = 26.2817$ Mbps, $C_{CT}'(G, H, I) = C_{CT}(G, H, I)/3 = 17.1$ Mbps, $C_{DT}'(I, J) = C_{DT}(I, J)/2 = 45.9182$ Mbps. As a result, the end-to-end throughput of $Flow_1$, $Flow_2$, and $Flow_3$ are min{61.189, 21.90} = 21.90 Mbps, min{36.5937, 26.2871} = 26.2817 Mbps and min{17.1, 45.9182} = 17.1 Mbps. The aggregate throughput of the whole network is 21.90 + 26.2817 + 17.1 = 65.2637 Mbps. Although there are three concurrent transmission flows, the aggregate throughput decreases about 10% compared with that in **Figure 3a**.

With the above-selected routes, we apply channel assignment to improve the network performance. In **Figure 3c**, we change the channel of node G, H, and I from the overloaded channel Ch_3 to the least-used one Ch_2, which reduces the number of interfering links on channel Ch_3 from three to two. The raw capacity of links on the paths of the three flows becomes $C_{DT}'(A, F) = C_{DT}(A, F)/2 = 30.5945$ Mbps, $C_{DT}'(F, K) = C_{DT}(F, K)/2 = 32.9909$ Mbps, $C_{DT}'(D, B) = C_{DT}(D, B)/2 = 36.5937$ Mbps, $C_{DT}'(B, E) = C_{DT}(B, E)/2 = 39.4226$ Mbps, $C_{CT}'(G, H, I) = C_{CT}(G, H, I)/2 = 25.6621$ Mbps, $C_{DT}'(I, J) = C_{DT}(I, J)/2 = 45.9182$ Mbps. As a result, the end-to-end throughput of $Flow_1$, $Flow_2$, and $Flow_3$ are 30.594, 36.5937, and 25.6621 Mbps, respectively. The aggregate throughput of the three flows in the network is 30.5945 + 36.5937 + 25.6621 = 92.8503 Mbps. The performance is improved almost 42% compared with that in **Figure 3b**.

Based on the above channel assignment, transmitter nodes would further check whether there exists a better relay node which can be utilized to obtain a better cooperative capacity gain. As shown in **Figure 3d**, node G can select node L instead of H as the relay node to further improve the performance. The available capacity of cooperative transmission can be calculated as $C_{CT}'(G, L, I) = C_{CT}(G, L, I)/2 = 66.5462/2 = 33.2731$ Mbps. As a result, the end-to-end throughput of $Flow_1$, $Flow_2$, and $Flow_3$ are 30.594, 36.5937, and 33.2731 Mbps. After relay adjustment, the aggregate throughput of the whole network is 30.5945 + 36.5937 + 33.2731 = 100.4613 Mbps, which is nearly 1.5 times that in **Figure 3b**.

Existing studies have demonstrated that the joint optimization problem of routing and channel assignment in multi-radio multi-channel wireless network is NP [27], the joint optimization problem of relay selection and cooperative routing is also NP [19]. Compared to the above problems where each considers only two issues, our problem considers three issues and can be generally proven to be NP-hard. To solve the problem, we propose a solution framework which is formed with three important components. In the following sections, we introduce the detailed algorithms for each part.

First, to obtain cooperative gain and reduce co-channel interference, every node periodically calculates the routing metric of CACU (contention-aware channel utilization). Based on this metric, when new flow arrives, an interference-aware cooperative routing algorithm is run to find the cooperative routing path and select MR and CR nodes along the path.

Second, to adapt to dynamic traffic changes, every node periodically measures the channel condition and calculates TACC metric. When a node's working channel is detected to be overloaded according to the TACC value, a dynamic channel-adjustment algorithm is triggered to switch the highly loaded channel to a lightly loaded one to relieve the co-channel interference.

Third, as channel adjustment changes the network topology, a local path segment and relay adjustment algorithm are followed by switching the flow traffic to a new path segment locally according to the new topology.

4. Cooperative route

To quantify the available capacity of a link, we first introduce a new routing metric. Based on the metric, we propose an interference-aware cooperative routing algorithm to better exploit the benefit of cooperative diversity.

There are several existing routing metrics proposed for multi-hop wireless networks. Hop count is a basic routing metric widely used. To further consider the wireless channel condition and interference, several improved metrics are also proposed, including ETX, WCETT, MIC, CCM [27], and MIPC [28]. The above routing metrics target for one-to-one direct transmissions between two nodes in conventional wireless networks. In cooperative wireless networks, the routing metric should consider multiple-to-one cooperative transmissions. As a cooperative transmission involves three links, it may cause more interference in the network, thus reducing the transmission performance. To facilitate the finding of more efficient cooperative routing path for higher throughput, the routing metric should concurrently consider the transmission mode selection and interference impact. To characterize radio transmissions in the presence of interference and identify the co-channel interference links of a given link, two receiver-driven interference models are proposed in the literature, the physical model [29] and the protocol model [30].

Our design does not depend on a specific model used. For the convenience of presentation and design, we simply apply a protocol model to illustrate our algorithms in this chapter. We consider link $l_{AB}^{Ch_i}$ to be the co-channel interference link of another link $l_{CD}^{Ch_i}$ if A and B work on the same channel of C and D, and at least one of node pairs (A,C), (A,D), (B,C), and (B,D) is within the interference range. A cooperative transmission may involve three nodes. We consider cooperative link $l_{AB(R)}^{Ch_i}$ to interfere with another link $l_{CD}^{Ch_i}$ if A, B, and R work on the same channel of C and D, and at least one of node pairs (A,C), (A,D), (B,C), (B,D), (R,C), and (R,D) is within the interference range.

If a node x transmits data to a node y through the direct transmission, the available capacity $C_{DT_a}(x, y, Ch_i)$ of the direct transmission link $l_{xy}^{Ch_i}$ is equal to the link capacity $C_{DT}(x, y)$ (calculated using Eq. (1)) deducted by the traffic load of its co-channel interference links:

$$C_{\mathrm{DT}_a}(x, y, Ch_i) = C_{\mathrm{DT}}(x, y) - \sum_{j \in I_{Ch_i}(l)} t(j), \tag{4}$$

where $t(j)$ is the traffic load on link j, $I_{Ch_i}(l)$ is the set of co-channel interference links of $l_{xy}^{Ch_i}$. Similarly, if node x transmits data to node y with the help of relay z, the available capacity $C_{CT_a}(x, z, y, Ch_i)$ of a cooperative transmission link $l_{xy(z)}^{Ch_i}$ can be calculated as

$$C_{CT_a}(x, z, y, Ch_i) = C_{CT}(x, z, y) - \sum_{j \in I_{Ch_i}(l)} t(j), \tag{5}$$

where $C_{CT}(x, z, y)$ is the capacity of the link $l_{xy(z)}^{Ch_i}$ (calculated using Eq. (2)), $I_{Ch_i}(l)$ is the set of co-channel interference links, and $t(j)$ denotes the traffic load on link j.

Therefore, the available capacity of a link (x, y, Ch_i) can be defined as the maximum available capacity among all possible transmission modes

$$\begin{aligned} CACU(x, y, Ch_i) = \max\Big\{ & C_{DT_a}(x, y, Ch_i), \max_z\Big\{ C_{CT_a}(x, z, y, Ch_i) \\ & : z \in N_{Ch_i}(x) \text{ and } N_{Ch_i}(y)\Big\}\Big\}, \end{aligned} \tag{6}$$

where $N_{Ch_i}(x)$ and $N_{Ch_i}(y)$ denote the set of neighbors of nodes x and y on the channel Ch_i. Obviously, $CACU(x, y, Ch_i) = C_{DT_a}(x, y, Ch_i)$ if the available capacity of direct transmission is larger than the available capacity of the cooperative transmission, otherwise, $CACU(x, y, Ch_i) = \max_z\left\{ C_{CT_a}(x, z, y, Ch_i) : z \in N_{Ch_i}(x) \text{ and } N_{Ch_i}(y) \right\}$. Multiple radios on a node are generally assigned with orthogonal channels. A pair of nodes x and y may have multiple channels to be the same. Based on Eq. (6), the routing metric of link (x, y) is defined as the maximum available capacity among all common channels as follows:

$$CACU(x, y) = \max_{Ch_i \in \omega(x) \cap \omega(y)} CACU(x, y, Ch_i), \tag{7}$$

where $w(x)$ and $w(y)$ denote the working channel set of nodes x and y, respectively. CACU metric in Eq. (7) captures the interference cost from both direct transmission and cooperative transmission. Therefore, CACU can be applied to facilitate finding a transmission path with lower interference thus higher capacity. Based on the metric, a node x can decide that it will take direct transmission or cooperative transmission, and determine the channel to use for transmission. In the case that a cooperative transmission is needed, the selected relay node will be informed.

In this chapter, we modified ad hoc on-demand distance vector (AODV) routing to implement our distributed interference-aware cooperative routing algorithm to establish the maximum capacity path while considering the flow routing and relay selection, as shown in Algorithm 1. The derived CACU metric is applied to construct the cooperative path. When a source has data to transmit but does not have a path to the destination, it broadcasts a route request (RREQ) for that destination. When an intermediate node receives RREQ, if it is the destination or has a current route to the destination, it generates a route reply (RREP). Otherwise, the node needs to rebroadcast the RREQ with a set of parameters inserted: the CACU metric for each of its outgoing link is calculated based on Eq. (7), and the maximum capacity from the source to itself is calculated based on Algorithm 1 in **Figure 4**.

Algorithm 1 Interference aware cooperative routing

Input: A newly arrival flow with the source s and the destination d

Output: Source s finds the cooperative routing path to the destination with each next hop's MR/CR relay and its transmission mode

For source node s**.**

When s intends to send packets to a destination d, it checks its routing table to see whether it has a valid path to d.
If so, it begins to send packet to the next hop towards the destination; otherwise, it searches for the path to the destination as follows.
for each neighbor node z of s **do**
  according to Eq(7), node s calculates the outgoing $link(s, z)$'s CACU metric which indicates the available capacity from s to z, denoted as P_{sz}, inserts P_{sz} into RREQ.
end for
Insert $P_s = +\infty$ into RREQ, where P_s denotes the maximum end-to-end capacity from s to s, broadcast the RREQ.

For intermediate node x **receiving a RREQ from node** y**.**

From RREQ message received, node x obtains P_y (the maximum end-to-end capacity from s to y), and P_{yx} (the available capacity from y to x). Node x calculates the maximum end-to-end capacity from s to x following $P_x = \min(P_{yx}, P_y)$.
if node x has received this RREQ before and $P_x \leq P_{x'}$, where $P_{x'}$ is the maximum end-to-end capacity from s to x which is maintained and updated at node x when the node receives the RREQ before **then**
  node x drops the RREQ.
else if node x is not the destination and does not have a current route to the destination **then**
  node x updates the maximum end-to-end capacity from s to x by using P_x.
  for each neighbor z of x **do**
    according to Eq(7), node x calculates its outgoing $link(x, z)$'s CACU metric, denoted as P_{xz}, inserts P_{xz} into RREQ.
  end for
  Insert the maximum end-to-end capacity from s to x, P_x into RREQ.
  Broadcast the RREQ.
else if node x is the destination or has a current route to the destination **then**
  node x generates a Route Reply (RREP).
end if

Figure 4. Algorithm 1: interference-aware cooperative routing.

5. Channel adjustment

As shown in the motivation example of Section 3, the channel adjustment can reduce co-channel interference and thus increase the aggregate throughput. The main function of channel adjustment is to switch one node's working channel from an overloaded one to a lightly loaded one to obtain better throughput. For practical implementation of the channel adjustment in a cooperative wireless network, we need to answer two basic questions: (1) Which channel to switch to? (2) How to keep the network stable and well connected during the channel adjustment?

Before presenting the detailed channel-adjustment algorithm, we first introduce a traffic-aware channel condition metric (TACC) to evaluate the channel load condition. The TACC of node i on channel Ch_m is defined as the channel utilization calculated as the summation of the co-channel traffic load within this node's two hops:

$$TAC\,C_i(Ch_m) = \sum_{j \in N_{Ch_m}(i)} \left(t(l_{ij}^{Ch_m}) + \sum_{k \in N_{Ch_m}(j)} t(l_{jk}^{Ch_m}) \right), \tag{8}$$

where $N_{Ch_m}(i)$ is node i's neighbor set on channel Ch_m, $t(l_{ij}^{Ch_m})$ denotes the traffic load on link $l_{ij}^{Ch_m}$, while j and k represent the one-hop and two-hop neighbors of node i, respectively. The average traffic conditions may be obtained by attaching the information with periodical topology maintenance messages such as Hello over two hops.

When a node finds that the TACC of a working channel exceeds a threshold θ_1, that is, $TAC\,C_i(Ch_m) \geq \theta_1$, it will trigger a channel-adjustment process. The node needs to identify a set of feasible candidate channels and selects the best one to switch to. To improve the network throughput with channel switching, the condition of the candidate channel Ch_b should be better than the condition of the current channel Ch_a. However, the channel adjustment may lead channel Ch_b to be overloaded and result in potential network instability. To avoid this problem, the following two conditions should be satisfied:

$$TACC_i(Ch_b) + Tload_i(Ch_a) \le \theta_2, \tag{9}$$

$$TACC_j(Ch_b) + Tload_i(Ch_a) \le \theta_2, \tag{10}$$

where node j is within two hops of node i, $Tload_i(Ch_a)$ is the total traffic load of all links on the original channel Ch_a, expressed as

$$Tload_i(Ch_a) = \sum_{j \in N_{Ch_a}(i)} t(l_{ij}^{Ch_a}). \tag{11}$$

We set θ_2 in Eq. (9) to $\theta_2 = 0.9 * \theta_1$ so that the TACC of the new channel after the channel switching is less than 90% of TACC trigger threshold to avoid another channel switching and maintain the network stability.

Figure 5 shows an example of channel-adjustment procedure. There are four flows in the network, $F_1(A \to I)$, $F_2(A \to L)$, $F_3(A \to D)$, and $F_4(B \to J)$. When node A finds that Ch_2 is overloaded, it tries to find another channel to switch to. If node A uses Ch_1 as the new channel, then nodes K, B, and F need to switch to Ch_1 to get connected with node A. This will change the traffic load of F_1, F_2 and F_3 on original links $l_{AK}^{Ch_2}$, $l_{AB}^{Ch_2}$, and $l_{AF}^{Ch_2}$ to the links $l_{AK}^{Ch_1}$, $l_{AB}^{Ch_1}$, and $l_{AF}^{Ch_1}$ on the new channel Ch_1. However, this will make Ch_1 overloaded and trigger another channel adjustment, which makes the network unstable. Therefore, Ch_1 is not the feasible candidate channel for node A because it does not satisfy condition in Eq. (9). Instead, according to Eq. (9), node A finds that Ch_3 is the candidate channel and the traffic load is switched from Ch_2 to Ch_3 as shown in **Figure 5c**.

Besides considering the condition in Eq. (9) to avoid network instability, to justify the extra channel switching overhead, the gains in terms of TACC should be larger than a given threshold θ_3:

$$\frac{Before\_TACC_i(Ch_a)}{After\_TACC_i(Ch_a)} \ge \theta_3, \tag{12}$$

where $Before\_TACC_i(Ch_a)$ is the original TACC value of the working channel Ch_a before channel switching, while $After\_TACC_i(Ch_a) = TACC_i(Ch_b) + Tload_i(Ch_a)$ is the TACC value of the working channel Ch_b after the channel switching.

Obviously, to obtain a positive benefit of channel switching, θ_3 in Eq. (12) should be larger than 1. Moreover, channel adjustment may involve a significant switching overhead such as switching delay and traffic interruption, and frequent channel switching will result in oscillation and severely impact the network performance. Therefore, θ_3 should be set by well considering the tradeoff between the switching overhead and the benefit of channel switching. According to Ref. [31], in our simulation, θ_3 is set to 1.2. That is, after the channel adjustment, the TACC of the new channel should be at least 20% less than that of the original one. Only

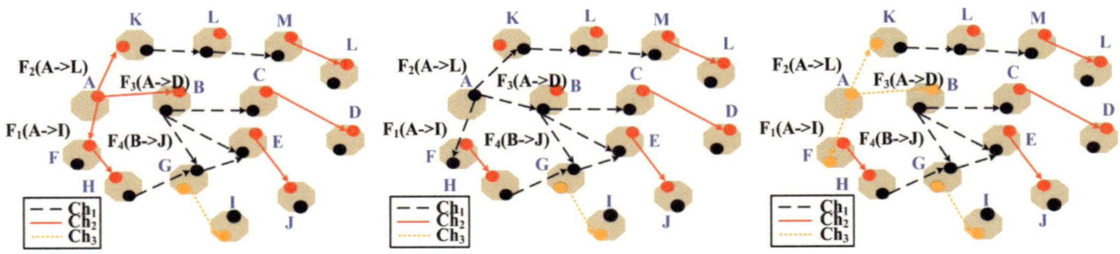

(a) Before channel adjustment (b) Switch A's channel to Ch_1 (c) Switch A's channel to Ch_3

Figure 5. An example of channel adjustment.

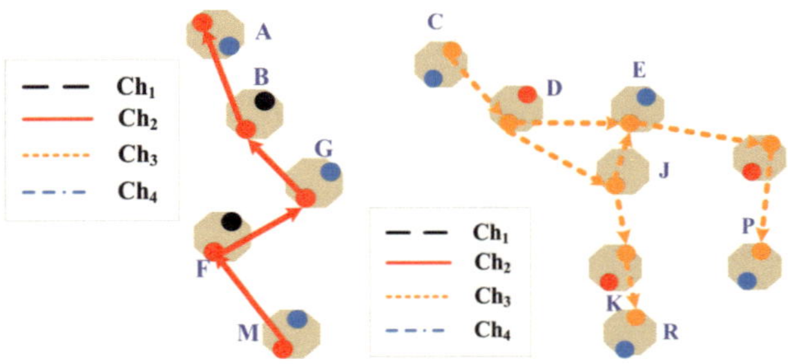

(a) Direct transmission (b) Cooperative transmission

Figure 6. Chain-puzzle problem.

when conditions of Eqs. (9), (10), and (12) are satisfied, the node can switch its working channel from Ch_a to Ch_b. To preserve the current flows' connectivity and stability, connectivity checking should be applied to further identify the feasible channel, which is discussed in the next subsection.

In an MRMC cooperative network, two nodes may have more than one pair of radios connected. If nodes i and j have two pairs of radios directly connected with each other, the channel adjustment does not impact their connectivity. If nodes i and j have only one radio connected with each other over a channel, the channel adjustment may interrupt the transmission of an active flow carried over the link (i, j). To maintain the connectivity of the active flow, the channel switching may be carried by a chain of nodes, with each node on the chain having only a single common channel. We define this problem as *chain puzzle*.

Cooperative transmission may be more prone to the chain-puzzle problem. **Figure 6** gives two examples to illustrate the chain-puzzle problem under direct transmission and cooperative transmission, respectively. In **Figure 6a**, assume that flow $F_1(M \rightarrow A)$ transmits over the link between nodes M and F using channel Ch_2, if the channel needs to be switched to Ch_3, node F's single-channel neighbor G must switch to Ch_3. Similarly, after node G switches its channel, node G's single-channel neighbor B has to switch to Ch_3 too, which will also lead channel switching from node A and thus result in the chain-puzzle problem. In **Figure 6b**, D, E, and J work together for cooperative transmission. Assume that nodes C and D currently transmitting over channel Ch_3 want to switch to Ch_1, nodes E and J are D's single-channel neighbors. To maintain the flow's connectivity, nodes E, J should switch channel from Ch_3 to Ch_1. As a result, K, R, Q, and P also need to switch their working channel from Ch_3 to Ch_1. Chain puzzle again happens.

Algorithm 2 The Chain puzzle checking algorithm

Input: A candidate channel Ch_i, channel adjustment triggering node A, and its set of upstream and downstream one-hop neighbors $N_{Ch_m}(A)$ on old channel Ch_m, the set of neighbor nodes within node A's two hops, denoted as $N_{two}(A)$.
Output: Whether candidate channel Ch_i is feasible candidate channel.

for node j in $N_{Ch_m}(A)$ **do**
  According to connectivity rule 1 and connectivity rule 2, node j identifies its two-hop neighbors which should switch their working channels to Ch_i when node j switches its working channel from Ch_m to Ch_i. Put such nodes into node set $N_{temp}(j)$.
  Node j sends the node set $N_{temp}(j)$ to node A
  if node A finds $N_{temp}(j)$ is not a subset of $N_{two}(A)$ **then**
    Channel switching will propagate beyond the two hops of node A and results in the chain puzzle problem.
    Ch_i is not a feasible channel, return False.
  end if
end for
Return True.

Algorithm 3 Feasible channel selection algorithm

Input: The orthogonal channels available, channel adjustment triggering node A and its overloaded working channel Ch_a.
Output: The selected channel for node A to switch to

Find channel Ch_b among orthogonal channels available that satisfies $TACC_i\,(Ch_b) + Tload_i\,(Ch_a) \leq \theta_2$, $TACC_j\,(Ch_b) + Tload_i\,(Ch_a) \leq \theta_2$, and $\frac{Before\_TACC_i(Ch_a)}{After\_TACC_i(Ch_b)} \geq \theta_3$ as the candidate feasible channel, and insert Ch_b into the feasible channel set.
Sort the candidate feasible channels in the descending order in a List according to the value of $\frac{Before\_TACC_i(Ch_a)}{After\_TACC_i(Ch_b)}$.
for Ch_i in List **do**
  According to connectivity rule 1 and connectivity rule 2, check whether Ch_i may cause chain puzzle by applying Algorithm 2.
  if chain puzzle does not happen under Ch_i **then**
    Ch_i is the selected feasible channel to switch to, and return Ch_i.
  end if
end for

Figure 7. Algorithm 2: the chain-puzzle-checking algorithm and Algorithm 3: feasible channel selection algorithm.

Chain-puzzle checking becomes an important issue in channel-adjustment procedure because chain puzzle may cause a number of practical problems. First, a large number of nodes may be involved in a channel switch when chain puzzle happens, which could result in a high overhead. Second, it is difficult to synchronize the switching action among all nodes involved because the signaling used for negotiation needs to propagate through many hops. In the worst case, this may result in flow transmission interruption. Therefore, before a node switches its working channel, chain puzzle should be checked to identify feasible candidate channel to avoid switching channel sequentially, and maintain the network's stability. To facilitate chain-puzzle checking, we propose two different connectivity rules according to different transmission modes:

Connectivity Rule 1: if any node pair of a direct transmission link passed by an active flow is originally connected, the node pair should remain connected after the channel switching.

Connectivity Rule 2: if any three nodes in an active cooperative transmission are originally connected, they should remain directly connected under a new channel.

Based on the above two connectivity rules, we propose a local two-hop chain-puzzle-checking sub-algorithm, as shown in Algorithm 2 of **Figure 7**. When node *A* checks a new channel Ch_i and finds that (through the communication with its neighbor which needs to switch channel with it) there exists a node which is not within its two-hop distance but also needs to switch channel to preserve the connectivity of the current flows, the chain puzzle may happen and Ch_i is not a feasible channel for channel adjustment. The results of chain-puzzle-checking algorithm depend on the topology of the network. Based on the chain-puzzle-checking algorithm, the feasible channel selection algorithm can be presented as in Algorithm 3 of **Figure 7**.

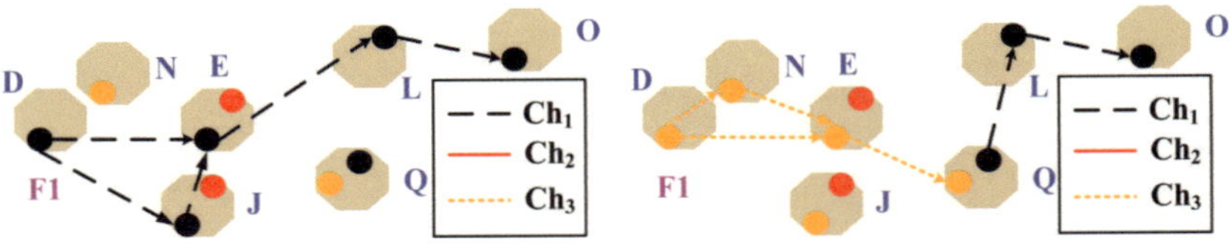

(a) Initial routing and relay assignment (b) Routing and relay adjustment

Figure 8. Local path adaptation and relay adjustment.

Algorithm 4 Local path adaptation and relay adjustment algorithm

Input: Channel adjustment triggering node A, the set of active flows which pass through node A, denoted as S. Node A's set of upstream and downstream two-hop neighbors in current active flows on the original routing paths, denoted as $u(S)$ and $d(S)$, respectively.

Output: Updated path segments and relay selections around node A for active flows

1: According to Eq.(7), node A and its one-hop neighbor nodes, and nodes in $u(S)$ and their one-hop neighbor nodes update their outgoing links' CACU metric, identify the selected transmission mode, relay and working channel for these links according to CACU value.

2: Applying the cooperative routing algorithm in Algorithm 1, find the local cooperative path segments with updated relays from A to its two-hop downstream nodes in $d(S)$, and from node A's two-hop upstream nodes in $u(S)$ to A .

Figure 9. Algorithm 4: local path adaptation and relay adjustment algorithm.

6. Local routing and relay adjustment

After channel adjustment, the network topology may change. To make flow transmissions continuous under the new topology, some flows may need to adapt their path segments, channels, or relays locally.

As shown in **Figure 8a**, an active flow $F_1(D \rightarrow O)$ exists in the network with its original route $F_1(D \rightarrow O) = D \xrightarrow{Ch_1} E(J) \xrightarrow{Ch_1} L \xrightarrow{Ch_1} O$. After nodes D, E, and J adjust their working channel from Ch_1 to Ch_3, nodes E and L are not directly connected. Thus, flow F_1 should switch its path locally from $E \xrightarrow{Ch_1} L$ to $E \xrightarrow{Ch_3} Q \xrightarrow{Ch_1} L$. Moreover, after D and E switch their working channel from Ch_1 to Ch_3, besides node J, node N may have the opportunity to support cooperative transmission and provide a higher cooperative gain. As a result, node D would select node N as the relay node instead of J. To make the network stable, the path adaptation and relay adjustment should be performed locally and the corresponding traffic flows should also switch to new path segments. Based on the cooperative routing algorithm in Algorithm 1, we design a local path adaptation and relay adjustment algorithm as shown in Algorithm 4 of **Figure 9**.

7. Completed solution

The complete algorithm of joint cooperative routing, channel adjustment, and relay selection is shown in Algorithm 5 of **Figure 10**. To handle the dynamic wireless environment, nodes in the network execute the algorithm locally as follows.

When a new flow arrives, the interference-aware cooperative routing algorithm is applied to find the cooperative routing path with the maximum end-to-end available capacity and with the MR and CR relays selected along the path. Every node periodically evaluates the traffic conditions of a channel by calculating the TCAA metric according to Eq. (8) and checking whether its working channel is overloaded. If so, the node first applies Algorithm 3 to identify

Algorithm 5 Complete algorithm of joint cooperative routing, channel assignment, and relay selection

When a new flow arrives
Apply interference-aware cooperative routing in Algorithm 1 to find the cooperative transmission path with MR and CR relays selected along the path.
When the TACC timer expires at a node i
Node i calculates TACC metric for its working channels following Eq.(8).
for Ch_m in $w(i)$, where $w(i)$ is the set of node i's working channel **do**
  if $TACC_i(Ch_m) \geq \theta_1)$ **then**
    Apply Algorithm 3 to identify the feasible channel for channel adjustment, let Ch_a be the feasible channel selected.
    Set node i's channel adjustment timer equal to $\frac{1}{TACC_i(Ch_m)}$.
    When the channel adjustment timer expires, node i switches its working channel to Ch_a, and then applies Algorithm 4 to complete local path segment adaptation and relay adjustment for all active flows passing node i
  end if
end for

Figure 10. Algorithm 5: complete algorithm of joint cooperative routing, channel assignment, and relay selection.

the feasible channel to switch to. Then, the channel adjustment will be triggered, which is followed by the local path adaptation and relay adjustment through Algorithm 4 for uninterrupted transmissions and better performance.

If each node independently makes a local channel-adjustment decision, multiple channel-adjustment requests may be received simultaneously by a node, which either leads to request message collisions or inconsistent requests (if all messages are successfully received). To reduce the chance of simultaneous transmissions of channel-adjustment messages, we design a channel-adjustment timer which introduces a random delay before the message sending according to the channel load, and the timer can be set as follows:

$$T_{iCh_m} = \frac{1}{TACC_i(Ch_m)}. \tag{13}$$

From Eq. (13), obviously, the node with a higher channel load, that is, a larger TACC value, has a lower average timer value, thus an earlier chance of adjusting its overloaded channel. When the channel load is high, the data transmissions should be switched from an overloaded channel to a light-loaded channel. In Algorithm 5, the channel load is measured with the metric TACC and updated when the TACC timer goes off. A smaller TACC timer would allow for more frequent update of the TACC value at high measurement cost, while a larger TACC timer for smaller measurement cost would make the TACC metric less accurate. In this chapter, we set the TACC timer adaptively according to the traffic pattern in the network taking into account the tradeoff between the accuracy of TACC metric and the measurement cost. If the traffic load is high, the TACC timer reduces but remains above a minimum timeout value T_{min}. If the traffic load is low, the TACC timer increases but not beyond a maximum timeout value T_{max}. In this chapter, we set T_{min} = 20 ms and T_{max} = 300 ms according to the channel-monitoring duration mentioned in [32].

8. Simulation

In the simulation, unless otherwise specified, the simulation setting is as follows. Thirty nodes are generated one by one in random locations in a 1000 × 1000 m area. Each new node is ensured to get connected with existing nodes in the network, and the initial channel assignment is done according to [26] to guarantee the connectivity of network to transmit possible flows over multiple hops. A node is equipped with two radio interfaces, and has the maximum transmission range set to 250 m. There are a total of 11 orthogonal channels, and the default number of flows in the network is set as $M = 5$.

Although ns-3 and Omnet++ are widespread simulator, cooperative communication is a physical layer technique, and can be very hard to simulate in ns-3 and Omnet++ if it is not completely impossible. Following the simulation setup in Refs. [17, 19], we evaluate the performance of our proposed algorithm through extensive simulations using MATLAB. Specifically, following the parameter setting in Ref. [19], we set the bandwidth of each channel to $W = 22$ MHz, the maximum transmission power at every node to 1 W. For simplicity, we assume that $h_{m,n}$ only considers the distance between nodes m and n and is given by $|h_{m,n}| = \|m, n\|^{-4}$, where $\|m, n\|$ is the distance (in m) between m and n and the path loss index is 4. We assume the variance of noise is 10^{-10} W at all nodes. TACC trigger threshold θ_1 is set to 200. We set θ_2 to $\theta_2 = 0.9 * \theta_1 = 180$ to help maintain network stability, and θ_3 to 1.2 to balance the switching overhead and benefit of channel switching.

We evaluate the effectiveness of our algorithms by comparing the results from six different implementation schemes. We implement two different cooperative transmission (CT) schemes. The first is our proposed Algorithm 5, denoted as CT_adjustment. In the second scheme, we apply the cooperative routing algorithm in Algorithm 1 to find the cooperative path, without applying channel adjustment or local path adaptation and relay adjustment, which is denoted as CT_No-adjustment. We also implement four additional schemes based on direct transmission (DT). The first DT scheme is denoted as DT_No-adjustment, where we use the available capacity calculated in Eq. (7) as the routing metric and apply Algorithm 1 to find the path with the maximum available capacity for each flow. In the second scheme, denoted as DT_ adjustment, channel and local path segment adjustment in Sections 5 and 6 are applied periodically to obtain better performance. The third and fourth schemes take two different routing metrics proposed in the literature to find the routing path: a HOP scheme, which uses hop count as routing metric and finds the shortest path, and an ETT scheme [27], which captures the packet transmission time in a time unit.

Two metrics are used to evaluate the performance. One is aggregate throughput which is the aggregative throughput of all flows. The other is minimum throughput, which is the minimum of all flows' throughput. Various factors affect the performance. We perform two set of simulations to analyze the effect of node density and number of orthogonal channel. As follows, we

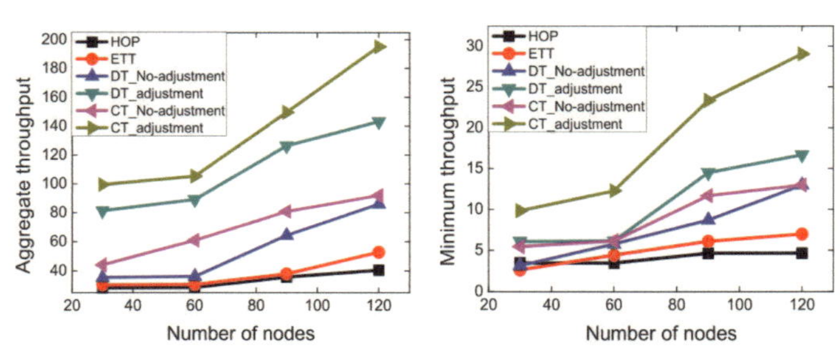

(a) Aggregate throughput (b) Minimum throughput

Figure 11. Throughput results under network with different node density.

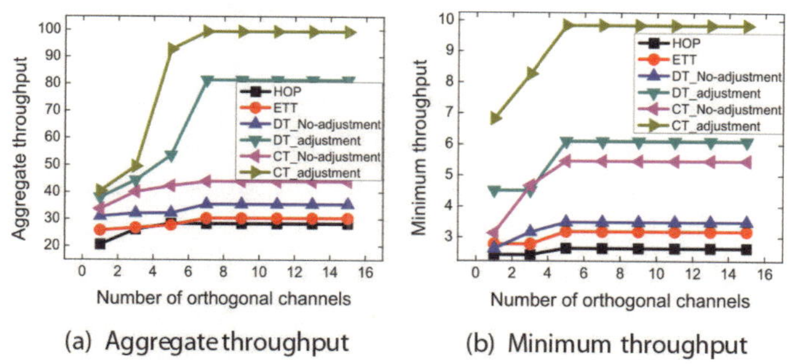

Figure 12. The impact of number of orthogonal channels.

show the simulation results, respectively. With the same topology and flows, we run the six schemes orderly to obtain the two metrics.

8.1. Impact of node density

To investigate how the node density impacts the network performance, we vary the number of nodes D from 30 to 120. When the number of nodes increases, the set of candidate relay nodes for cooperative relay (CR) and multi-hop relay (MR) becomes larger. Therefore, the aggregate rate and minimum rate under all routing schemes increase, as shown in **Figure 11**.

Among all the routing schemes, the aggregate throughput and the minimum throughput increase the fastest under our CT_adjustment. With well-designed algorithms, our CT_adjustment can more effectively exploit the resources of relay nodes and multiple channels to achieve high cooperative gain when the number of nodes is large. Our CT_adjustment has the largest aggregate throughput and minimum throughput. At the node density 120, the aggregate throughput of our CT_adjustment is 382, 270, 276, 127, 36, and 112% higher than those of HOP, ETT, DT_No-adjustment, DT-adjustment, CT_No-adjustment, and CT-adjustment, respectively. The minimum throughput of CT_adjustment is 527, 317, 235, 124, 74, and 124% higher than those of HOP, ETT, DT_No-adjustment, DT-adjustment, and CT_No-adjustment, respectively.

Although the performance under CT_No-adjustment is much better than that under DT_No-adjustment, the performance under DT_adjustment is better than that under CT_No-adjustment. As discussed in "Introduction", under CT_No-adjustment, although relay nodes can help to increase the capacity of a transmission pair, cooperative transmissions may also cause interference to more network nodes and consequently significant performance degradation. Compared with CT_No-adjustment, CT adjustment can obtain much larger cooperative transmission gain, which demonstrates the effectiveness of our algorithms in relieving the interference raised by cooperative relays. The performance gain is also attributed to our algorithms for channel adjustment and adaptation of local path segments and relays. By exploiting the MRMC technique, the co-channel interference is alleviated, which is the key reason for the throughput improvement.

8.2. Impact of the number of orthogonal channel

We vary the number of orthogonal channels from 1 to 15 in the network while setting other parameters to the default values. As shown in **Figure 12**, the aggregate network throughput and minimum flow throughput achieved by all the routing schemes increase when the number of orthogonal channels increases initially, while remaining the same when the number of channels is large enough for the tested five flows. As each node has only two radio interfaces and the traffic in the network is limited, extra channels cannot be fully utilized. Therefore, increasing the number of channels cannot unboundedly increase the performance of the routing schemes for the tested five flows. We observe that CT_adjustment can exploit available orthogonal channels to increase the throughput and achieve the best performance. When the number of channels is larger than 5, CT_adjustment achieves 251, 228, 180, 22, and 126% higher aggregate throughput compared to HOP, ETT, DT_No-adjustment, DT-adjustment, and CT_No-adjustment, respectively.

9. Conclusion

To fulfill the complete potential of cooperative transmission in MRMC cooperative networks, a solution is proposed where cooperative routing at the network layer, channel assignment at the MAC layer, and cooperative communication at the physical layer can work coherently together to maximize the throughput. The simulation results demonstrate that cooperative communication can achieve a large capacity gain in MRMC wireless networks under well-designed algorithms. Compared to direct transmission in multi-radio multi-channel, cooperative transmission in multi-radio multi-channel can increase the aggregate throughput more than 1.8 times when there are at least five orthogonal channels.

Acknowledgements

This work is supported by the National Natural Science Foundation of China under grant nos.6157218, 61472130, 71331001, and 71420107027, U.S. National Science Foundation under grant no. CNS 1526843, the Science and Technology Projects of Hunan Province (No. 2016JC2075), and the Research Foundation of Education Bureau of Hunan Province, China (No. 16C0047).

Author details

Kun Xie[1,*], Shiming He[2], Xin Wang[3], Dafang Zhang[1] and Keqin Li[4]

*Address all correspondence to: xiekun@hnu.edu.cn

1 College of Computer Science and Electronics Engineering, Hunan University, Changsha, China

2 School of Computer and Communication Engineering, Changsha University of Science and Technology, Changsha, China

3 Department of Electrical and Computer Engineering, State University of New York at Stony Brook, Stony Brook, USA

4 Department of Computer Science, State University of New York, New York, USA

References

[1] Xie K, Cao J, Wang X, Wen J. Optimal resource allocation for reliable and energy efficient cooperative communications. IEEE Trans. Wireless Commun. 2013;**12**(10):4994–5007. DOI: 10.1109/TWC.2013.081913.121709

[2] Xie K, Cao J, Wen J. Optimal relay assignment and power allocation for cooperative communications. J. Comput. Sci. Technol. 2013;**28**(2):343–356. DOI: 10.1007/s11390-013-1335-3

[3] Zhu Y, Zheng H. Understanding the impact of interference on collaborative relays. IEEE Trans. Mobile Comput. 2008;**7**(6):724–736. DOI: 10.1109/TMC.2007.70790

[4] Yang F, Huang M, Zhao M, Zhang S, Zhou W. Cooperative strategies for wireless relay networks with cochannel interference over time-correlated fading channels. IEEE Trans. Veh. Technol. 2013;**62**(6):3392–3408. DOI: 10.1109/TVT.2013.2242911

[5] Dehghan M, Ghaderi M, Goeckel D. On the performance of cooperative routing in wireless networks. In: INFOCOM Conf. Comput. Commun. Workshops; 15–19 March 2010; San Diego, CA, New York, NY: IEEE; 2010. pp. 1–5.

[6] Xie K, Xie K, He S, Zhang D, Wen J, Lloret J. Busy tone based channel access control for cooperative communication. Trans. Emerg. Telecommun. Technol. 2015;**26**(10): 1173–1188. DOI: 10.1002/ett.2856

[7] Lin T, Wu K, Yin G. Channel-hopping scheme and channel diverse routing in static multi-radio multi-hop wireless networks. IEEE Trans. Comput. 2015;**64**(1):71–86. DOI: 10.1109/TC.2013.199

[8] He S, Zhang D, Xie K, Qiao H, Zhang J. Channel aware opportunistic routing in multi-radio multi-channel wireless mesh networks. J. Comput. Sci. Technol. 2014;**39**(3):487–501. DOI:10.1007/s11390-014-1444-7.

[9] He S, Zhang D, Xie K, Qiao H, Zhang J. A distributed low-complexity channel assignment for opportunistic routing. China Commun. 2012;**11**:9–22.

[10] I. W. Group. IEEE Wireless LAN Medium Access Control (MAC) and Physical Layer (PHY) Specifications, IEEE Std 802.11-1997, 1997. DOI: 10.1109/IEEESTD.1997.85951

[11] I. 802.11a Working Group. Wireless LAN medium access control (MAC) and physical layer (PHY) specifications-Amendment 1: High-speed physical layer in the 5 GHz band. IEEE Std 802.11a-1999, 1999.

[12] Mansourkiaie F, Ahmed MH. Cooperative routing in wireless networks: a comprehensive survey. IEEE Commun. Surveys Tutor. 2015;**17**(2):604–626. DOI: 10.1109/COMST.2014.2386799

[13] Bai Z, Jia J, Wang C, Yuan D. Performance analysis of SNR-based incremental hybrid decode-amplify-forward cooperative relaying protocol. IEEE Trans. Commun. 2015; **63**(6): 2094–2106. DOI: 10.1109/TCOMM.2015.2427166

[14] Ding H, Costa DB, Liu W, Ge J. Enhancing cooperative diversity gains in dual-hop one-way/two-way AF relaying systems: a fully opportunistic role selection strategy. IEEE Trans. Veh. Technol. 2015;64(8): 3440–3457. DOI: 10.1109/TVT.2014.2356506

[15] Elhawary M, Haas Z. Energy-efficient protocol for cooperative networks. IEEE/ACM Trans. Netw. 2011;**19**(2):561–574. DOI: 10.1109/TNET.2010.2089803

[16] Xu H, Huang L, Qiao C, Zhang Y, Sun Q. Bandwidth power aware cooperative multipath routing for wireless multimedia sensor networks. IEEE Trans. Wireless Commun. 2012;**11**(4):1532–1543. DOI: 10.1109/TWC.2012.020812.111265

[17] Guo Y, Duan L, Zhang R. Optimal pricing and load sharing for energy saving with cooperative communications. IEEE Trans. Wireless Commun. 2016;**15**(2):951–964. DOI: 10.1109/TWC.2015.2480771

[18] Jayakody DNK, Flanagan MF. A soft decode–compress–forward relaying scheme for cooperative wireless networks. IEEE Trans. Veh. Technol. 2016;65(5):3033–3041. DOI: 10.1109/TVT.2015.2442459

[19] Jiang W, Kaiser T, Vinck AJH. A robust opportunistic relaying strategy for co-operative wireless communications. IEEE Trans. Wireless Commun. 2016;**15**(4):2642–2655. DOI: 10.1109/TWC.2015.2506574

[20] Nazari B, Jamalipour A. Contract-auction based distributed resource allocation for cooperative communications. IET Commun. 2016;10(9):1087–1095. DOI: 10.1049/iet-com.2015.0764

[21] Xie K, Wang X, Liu X, Wen J, Cao J. Interference-aware cooperative communication in multi-radio multi-channel wireless networks. IEEE Trans. Comput. 2016;**65**(5):1528–1542. DOI: 10.1109/TC.2015.2448089

[22] Xie K, Wang X, Wen J, Cao J. Cooperative routing with relay assignment in multi-radio multihop wireless networks. IEEE/ACM Trans. Netw. 2016;**24**(2):859–872. DOI: 10.1109/TC.2015.2448089

[23] Xie K, Li H, Wang X, He S, Wen J, Guizani M. Joint cooperative routing and channel assignment in multi-flow multi-hop wireless networks. In: IWCMC; 4–8 August. 2014; Nicosia. New York, NY: IEEE; 2014, p. 1188–1193.

[24] Qiao H, Zhang D, Xie K, Zhang J, He S. Power-bandwidth aware cooperative routing in multi-radio multi-channel wireless network. In: IEEE ISPA; 23-26 Aug; Tianjin China. New York, NY: IEEE; 2016, pp. 1342–1349.

[25] Qiao H, Zhang D, Xie K, Zhang J, He S. A distributed joint cooperative routing and channel assignment in multi-radio wireless mesh network. In: ICA3PP; 18–20 November 2015; Zhangjiajie China. Springer Verlag; 2015, pp. 552–566.

[26] Raniwala A, Gopalan K, Chiueh T-C. Centralized channel assignment and routing algorithms for multi-channel wireless mesh networks. ACM SIGMOBILE Mobile Comput. Commun. Rev. 2004; **8**(2):50–65. DOI: 10.1145/997122.997130

[27] Wu H, Yang F, Tan K, Chen J, Zhang Q, Zhang Z. Distributed channel assignment and routing in multiradio multichannel multihop wireless networks. IEEE J. Sel. Areas Commun. 2006; **24**(11): 1972–1983. DOI: 10.1109/JSAC.2006.881638

[28] He S, Xie K, Xie K, Li Z, Xu C. Interference-aware multi-source transmission. In: IEEE ISPA; 23-26 Aug; Tianjin China. New York, NY: IEEE; 2016, pp.1233-1240

[29] Gupta P, Kumar P. The capacity of wireless networks. IEEE Trans. Inf. Theory. 2000; **46**(2):388–404. DOI: 10.1109/18.825799

[30] Ma H, AlAzemi H, Roy S. A stochastic model for optimizing physical carrier sensing and spatial reuse in wireless ad hoc networks. In: IEEE Int. Conf. Mobile Adhoc Sensor Syst. Conf.; 7 November, 2005; Washington, DC. New York, NY: IEEE; 2005, pp. 615–622.

[31] Chen L, Zhang Q, Li M, Jia W. Joint topology control and routing in IEEE 802.11-based multiradio multichannel mesh networks. IEEE Trans. Veh. Technol. 2007; 56(5): 3123–3136. DOI: 10.1109/TVT.2007.900509

[32] Middleton G, Aazhang B. Relay selection for joint scheduling, routing and power allocation in multiflow wireless networks. In: 4th Int. Symp. Commun., Control Signal Process.; 3–5 March 2010; Limassol. New York, NY: IEEE; 2010, pp. 1–4.

Section 2

Future Trends

Chapter 5

MANET Network in Internet of Things System

Rasa Bruzgiene, Lina Narbutaite and
Tomas Adomkus

Additional information is available at the end of the chapter

http://dx.doi.org/10.5772/66408

Abstract

In the current world of technology, various physical things can be used for facilitation of a human work. That is why the Internet of Things,an innovative technology and a good solution which allows the connection of the physical things with the digital world through the use of heterogeneous networks and communication technologies, is used. The Internet of Things in smart environments interacts with wireless sensor network (WSN) and mobile ad-hoc network (MANET), making it even more attractive to the users and economically successful. Interaction between wireless sensor and mobile ad-hoc networks with the Internet of Things allows the creation of a new MANET-IoT systems and IT-based networks. Such the system gives the greater mobility for a user and reduces deployment costs of the network. However, at the same time it opens new challenging issues in its networking aspects as well. In this work, the authors propose a routing solution for the Internet of Things system using a combination of MANET protocols and WSN routing principles. The presented results of solution's investigation provide an effective approach to efficient energy consumption in the global MANET-IoT system. And that is a step forward to a reliable provision of services over global Future Internet infrastructure.

Keywords: MANET, IoT, Sensor, energy efficiency, dynamic routing

1. Introduction

The Internet of Things (IoT) is a part of the Future Internet paradigm, which rapidly changes the development of technologies as well as provision of services over different communication networks. The capability of objects (like physical or virtual things) to identify and communicate with each other at any time-evolving communication technologies gives the possibility to provide advanced services over global infrastructure (as Internet) in different areas of everyday life [1]. The interconnection of smart objects and its interoperability with global communications serve as a main idea incorporated in Internet of Things systems. Wireless sensor network (WSN) plays a main role in the IoT system as its components include sensing, acquiring of data, heterogeneous connectivity, data processing, etc. Mobile ad-hoc network (MANET) is a wireless, multi-hop, self-configuring network. Its each node operates as an end system and/or a router for other nodes in the network and is closely related to WSNs. The interaction between MANET and Internet of Things opens new ways for provision of services in smart environments and challenging issues in its networking aspects as well.

One of the important factors in such MANET-IoT systems is the energy balancing over nodes, since the IoT system is based mostly on many different wireless sensors and MANET protocols focus on selecting the shortest and efficient paths for transactions. A proper utilization of sensor's battery power is a significant key in maintaining network connectivity of a multi-hop wireless network. Due to this, many researchers are focusing on designing energy efficient routing protocols that prolong such network lifetime. Wireless network protocols like MANET cannot be used directly due to resource constraints of sensors' nodes, computational speed, human interface with node's devices and density of nodes in network. Therefore, it is a need of composite solution for routing over MANET-IoT networks, which can use efficiently residual energy of nodes and extend the network's lifetime.

In this chapter, the authors propose an algorithm of energy efficient and safe-weighted clustering routing for the mobile IoT system using a combination of MANET and WSN routing principles. Clustering is one method of making routing less complex, and for some sensor networks, more energy efficient. Such combination of MANET and WSN routing principles is able to increase the lifetime of sensors in the overall mobile Internet of Things system. It is important to decide how many cluster heads (CHs) are needed and which of the sensor nodes are going to act as cluster heads. MANET network nodes were chosen as a cluster head and a proactive routing protocol was used in such a way that it is possible to control and update a table of information about the state of the network. Nodes that rapidly lose its energy or that are left with low energy were identified and their workloads were limited for transactions. All investigations for the selection of a routing path over the MANET-IoT system were performed by using the MATLAB simulation platform.

This research work provides important key insights into the combination of MANET and WSN routing principles by increasing the lifetime of sensors in the overall Internet of Things system. The solution of routing optimization with an effective and efficient approach to energy consumption in the global MANET-IoT system is presented as main result of this work, which can help in accessibility and provision of services for a longer period of time over global Future Internet infrastructure.

2. Background

2.1. Mobile ad-hoc network (MANET)

The mobile ad-hoc networks (MANETS) are autonomously self-organized networks without fixed topology. In such a network, each node acts as both router and hosts at the same time.

http://dx.doi.org/10.5772/66408

All network nodes are equivalent to each other and can move out or join in the network freely. The mobile nodes that are in the radio range of each other can directly communicate and transfer the necessary information. All network nodes have a wireless interface to communicate with another node in the range. This kind of network is fully distributed and can work at any place without the help of any fixed infrastructure as access points or base stations. **Figure 1** shows the example of mobile ad-hoc network [2].

It can be assigned two multiple ad-hoc network types: (a) mobile ad-hoc network (MANET) and (b) mobile ad-hoc sensor network. A mobile ad-hoc sensor network has much wider sequences of operational, and at the same time needs a less complex setup procedure compared to typical sensor networks, which communicate directly with the centralized controller [3]. There are six main characteristics of MANETs [2]: distributed operation; multi-hop routing, autonomous terminal, dynamic topology, lightweight terminals, and shared physical medium.

MANET routing protocols can be categorized into three types:

1. Topology-based routing

   The routing types [3] are: (a) proactive routing protocols (routing table-based), (b) reactive routing protocols (demand based) are presented in **Figure 2** and (c) hybrid routing protocols. These protocols are the combination of proactive and reactive routing protocols. One of them is ZRP (zone routing protocol).

2. Location-based routing

   To make routing decision, location-based routing uses the actual position of nodes in any area. Location information can be obtained, for example, using global positioning system (GPS). Location-aided routing (LAR) protocol is an example of location-based routing.

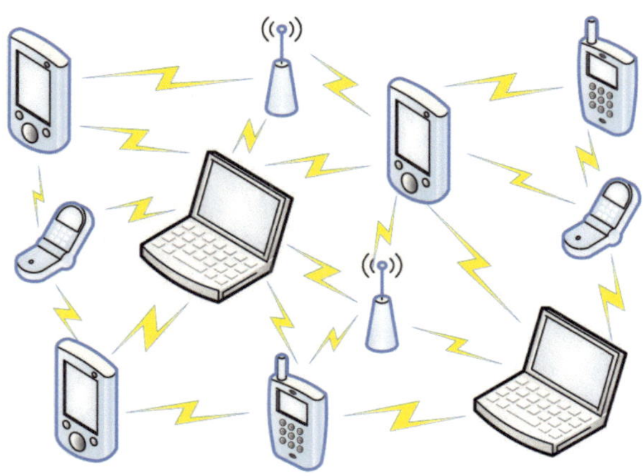

Figure 1. Example of mobile ad-hoc network.

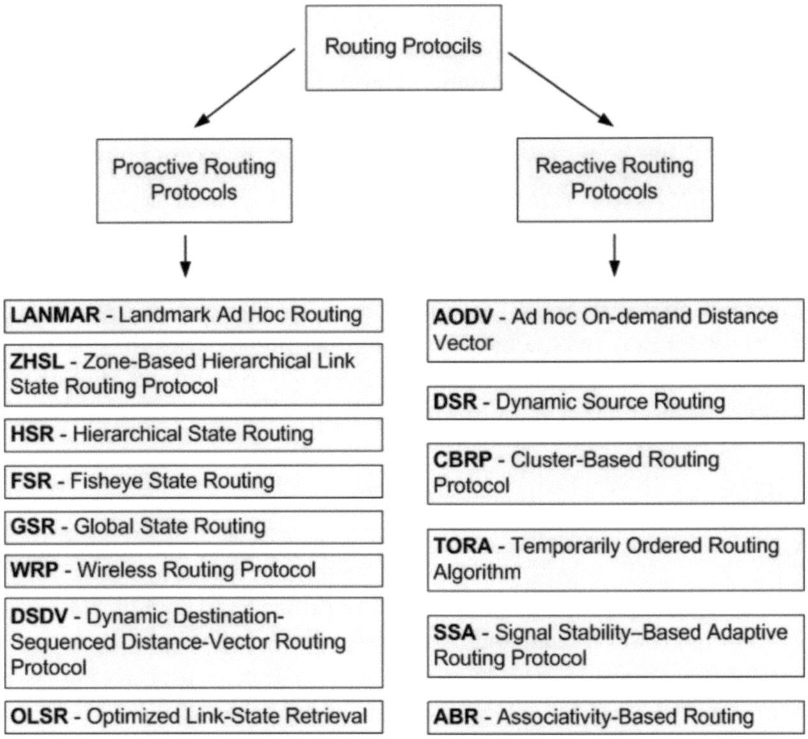

Figure 2. Proactive and reactive routing protocols.

3. Energy awareness-based routing

Each node in the network supports multiple entries of routing in routing tables. For choosing optimal route in the wireless medium, routing assessing power levels of network nodes is available. In this case, routing table corresponding to the power level of nodes and maintained by transferring hello messages in between nodes at the power level. The number of entries in routing table of nodes is corresponding to the number of nodes reachable by using the power level. Thus, the number of entries in routing tables gives the total number of network nodes [4].

2.2. The characterization of Internet of Things (IoT)

Today a human is surrounded by various things—from the smallest items to the gigantic objects. The need to "recruit" these things was a great reason for the connection of electronics, devices, with digital communications, using the Internet as a main medium for data transmission. The human is just as data traffic end user in such connection, as all communication, management and information exchange are processing among connected things and objects. The capability of real or virtual things and objects to be identifiable, to communicate with anything and to interact with anything lets to build networks of interconnected objects, end users or other entities in the global Internet network. So the term "Internet of Things" mainly

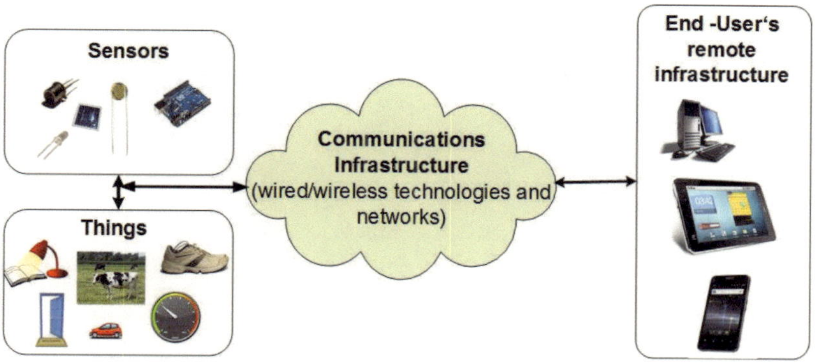

Figure 3. Global structure of Internet of Things system.

means the global infrastructure (**Figure 3**) of interconnected things, devices, or objects, which can communicate, actuate, exchange their information over Internet to the end users using the interaction between communication technologies and networks.

Internet of Things is the part of Future Internet (**Figure 4**) [5]. The concept of Future Internet connects the Internet of Users and Knowledge (IoUK), Internet of Networks (IoN), Internet of Services (IoS) and Internet of Things. IoUK is used for people's social gaming or users monitoring, IoN opens possibilities for unlimited connectivity of networks and IoS is use for provision of web-based services in the global smart industry. Broadly, Internet of Things covers the large potential of computing and communication capabilities into the objects, which can interoperate in global-integrated communication platforms. It serves as a bridge between the real things and digital, information world.

Sensors are the main elements that connect things, their data with remote end users. The sensors collect useful information for the end users data, convert it to digital format and transmit it to the other devices in IoT-based systems with the help of various existing wireless or wired technologies [6]. As sensors are well deployed and it quantity is growing rapidly in the world, it serves as main interface, connecting things, communications and end users. The selection of medium for the data transmission, processing of data routing over different heterogeneous networks are one of the major challenges in the IoT-based systems [7]. Wireless technologies,

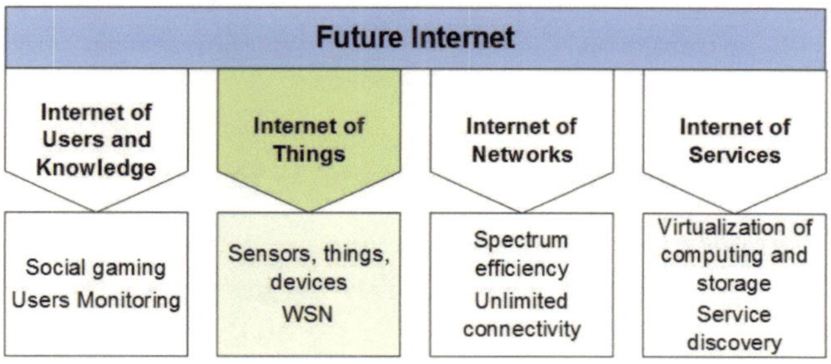

Figure 4. IoT in Future Internet concept.

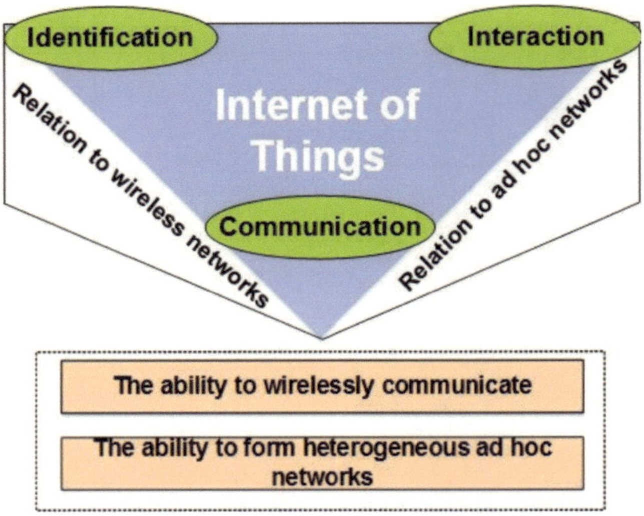

Figure 5. Internet of Things characteristics and it relation with wireless and ad-hoc networks.

ad-hoc wireless networks are the most effective and low-cost way to transmit data in Internet of Things systems. Furthermore, it perfectly solves human's need for the mobility and significantly reduces the cost of installation of such systems, comparing it with the deployment cost of wired technologies.

The main characteristics [8] of Internet of Things and its relation with wireless and ad-hoc networks are presented in **Figure 5**.

The things, which are in the Internet of Things system, are identified and relations among them are specified in the digital domain; it has the ability to communicate to each other using wireless technologies as well to form different ad-hoc wireless networks of interconnected things. Their sensing and actuating capabilities can be used for interaction with the surrounding environment. However, IoT-based system needs to support main factors as heterogeneity of things and devices, efficient energy usage, interoperability and data management as well as security and privacy [8]. The capability of the IoT systems to support these factors ensures IoT application in different areas of smart cities [9]: healthcare, energy, buildings, transport, industry, etc. Moreover, the key technologies for Internet of Things-based systems' application in these areas are wireless sensor networks (WSNs) and MANETs [10, 11].

2.3. Internet of Things interaction with MANET and WSN

Possibilities of wide application of Internet of Things systems in different areas are directly dependent on the opportunities of interoperability between different communication technologies and networks in smart environments. The growth of sensors quantity leads to the increasing need of humans for a remote monitoring of different processes in smart environments. And this is possible by widespread deployment of wireless sensor networks (WSN).

Basically, WSN is a network, which consists of different sensors that are capable autonomously to read information from the object, which is been measured, to handle sensed data, temporarily store it and transfer sensed data to another network node, which is also a sensor. As WSN is a normally centralized network [12], so the data, sensed and transferred from other sensors, are transmitted to the central node, which is usually called the sink. In this manner, the wireless sensors are able to communicate with each other and thus open very wide usability opportunities of wireless sensor networks in IoT systems. Wireless sensor networks mainly are the basic element in the global Internet of Things system, as sensors have the ability to gather information from different things and transmit it over the network. However, the reliability of IoT systems is highly dependent on the power consumption and scalability of WSN [13]. The sensors should transmit measured data so efficiently to the sink, that the energy of their battery would be used at the minimum level. Due to this, the wireless sensor network should be constrained that it can easily accommodate changes in the network. This is related to the lifetime of WSN as well, as low or empty battery leads to the death of sensors. In this way, the routing principles and methods are very important and challenging issue of WSN as data should be transmitted by another sensor, eliminating dead sensor from the routing path. And it should be done with respect to Quality of Service (QoS) over wireless sensor networks [14].

Wireless sensor network in general is similar to a mobile ad-hoc network (MANET), since both are self-organized and multi-hopped networks. However, the topology of MANET is more changeable than WSN. MANET protocols can let it to act as a WSN backbone [15] and access wireless sensor network's nodes as well exchange information with WSN about MANET entry points [10]. Due to the task to use sensors' energy efficiency during the data transmission and to reduce data processing time by selecting proper routing protocols and principles, it is a demand for the convergence of MANET and WSN networks. Also, these two networks can enable more effective and reliable cross-network routing in the Internet of Things context. The intersection of MANET, WSN and Internet of Things the authors called as a MANET-IoT system, which is discussed in detail in Section 3. **Figure 6** presents the main aspects of interaction between Internet of Things, wireless sensor networks and mobile ad-hoc networks.

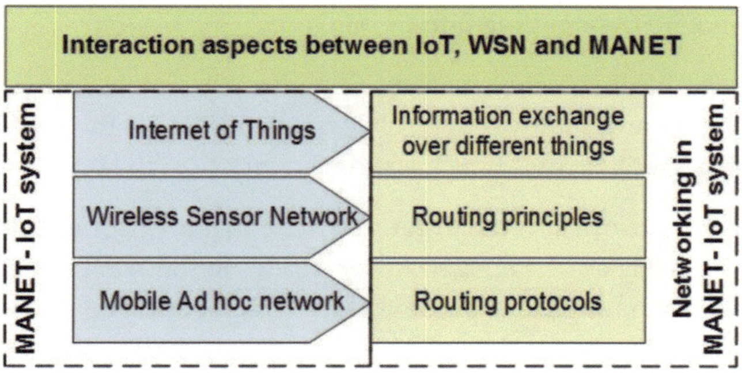

Figure 6. Intersection of IoT, WSN and MANET.

Networking in the MANET-IoT system is based on the routing protocols of MANET, routing principles of wireless sensor network and data sensing from things, handling and processing using Internet of Things. In general, networking of such the system is a very challenging regarding routing aspects. Also, it is related to system mobility and limited resources of all sensors in the network. MANET protocols (most of them) are designed with the focus on QoS [16, 17] and routing in wireless sensor networks is focused on the efficient energy consumption of network nodes [18]. The connection of different things with limited features to the Internet and interaction with different wireless and mobile ad-hoc networks must guarantee connectivity, accessibility and reliability of the MANET-IoT system in smart environments. The solutions for the routing protocols of ad-hoc network modification in order to fulfil the requirements of the Internet of Things were presented by Tian and Hou [19]. Routing principles were changed by integrating IPv6 [20]. However, the interaction of Internet of Things with MANET and WSN requires new, optimized solution for data routing in such the MANET-IoT system. The authors proposed an algorithm for data routing, which is mainly focused on energy efficiency and safe weighted clustering in the MANET-IoT system. The authors' proposed solution is described in Sections 3 and 4.

3. Proposed solution for data routing in the MANET-IoT system

3.1. Mathematical model for calculation of network energy cost function

Sensors establish and maintain routes can proactively or reactively. Proactive protocols periodically monitor peer connectivity to ensure the ready availability of any path among active nodes. Sensors advertise their routing state to the entire network to maintain a common or partially complete topology of the network. Reactive protocols establish paths only upon request. For MANET sensor network in the IoT system information routing we use combination of two routing principles: OLSR (optimized link-state retrieval) and LEACH (low energy adaptive clustering hierarchy).

Clustering network is efficient and scalable way to organize WSN. Clustering is the method by which sensor nodes in a network organize themselves into hierarchical structures. By doing this, sensor nodes can use battery power more efficiently. A cluster head (CH) is responsible for conveying any information gathered by the nodes in its cluster and may aggregate and compress the data before transmitting it to the sink.

LEACH selects cluster head randomly among all nodes completely. Using our propose algorithm of energy efficient and safe-weighted clustering routing for the mobile IoT system, the cluster head is a node that in actual time has more energy than the threshold value.

The sensing range of a sensor is the maximum distance that a sensor can sense. To form clusters, sensor nodes first elect a CH for each cluster. Nodes in the WSN which are not CHs find the closest CH within the range and become cluster members. The nodes in a cluster only communicate with one another and the CH. The number of CH can be different for every network topology. The propose algorithm implementing dynamical CH rotation that allows

http://dx.doi.org/10.5772/66408

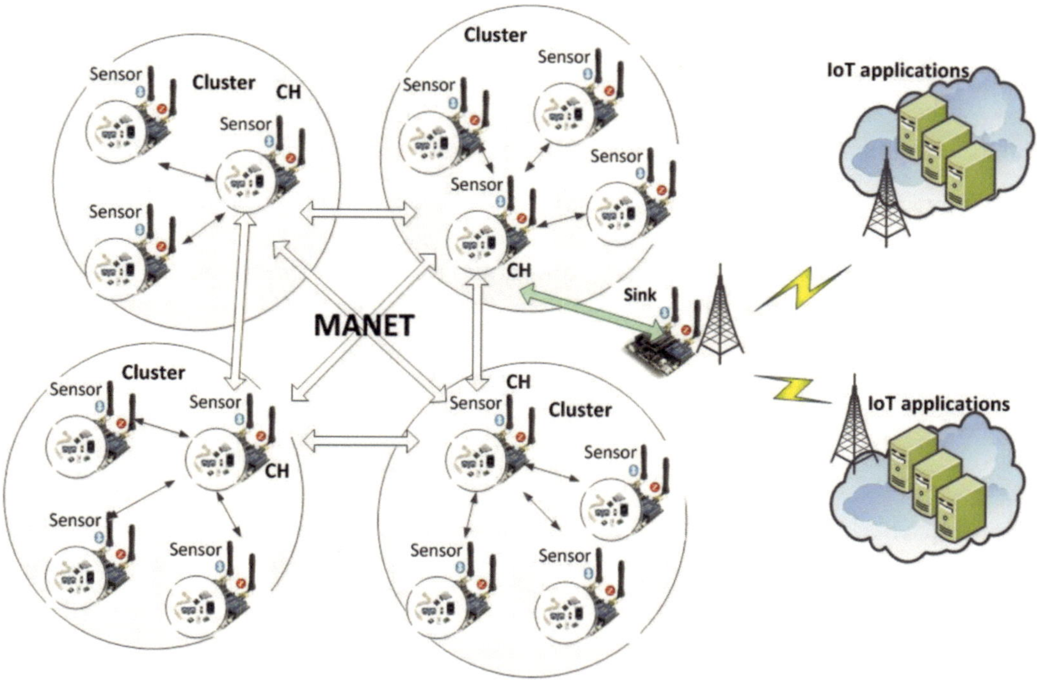

Figure 7. MANET-IoT network with a cluster topology.

us to distribute the workload CH across the mobile MANET-IoT system and extend overall lifetime of our system.

The MANET-IoT network with a cluster topology is shown in **Figure 7**. Sensors are grouped into clusters and individual sensors sense data and transmit to cluster heads (CH). Cluster heads aggregate this data and then forward, depending on the tree structure, to the base station or sink node. We assume that each sensor senses L bits and transmit to CH.

The energy consumed by a sensor node consists of these parts [21]:

- microcontroller processing,
- radio transmission and receiving,
- transient energy,
- sensor sensing,
- sensor logging and actuation.

The sensor energy dissipation for sensing activity and logging is evaluated in references [22, 23]

$$E_s = L * V * I_s * T_s, \tag{1}$$

$$E_{\log} = \frac{L * V}{8}\left(I_r * T_r + I_w * T_w\right), \quad (2)$$

where L = packet size, V = supply voltage, I_s = current required for sensing, I_r = current required for reading, I_w = current required for writing, T_s = time duration required for sensing, T_r = time duration required for reading, T_w = time duration required for writing.

We assume that energy used by CH is higher than that of a normal sensor node, because of additional data aggregation tasks per cycle from other sensors in parallel. Therefore, use coefficient φ, which indicate how much CH consumes more energy than a regular sensor node and these coefficients are >1. Then we have

$$E_{s(CH)} = \varphi_1 * E_s \quad (3)$$

$$E_{\log(CH)} = \varphi_2 * E_{\log}. \quad (4)$$

The coefficient φ_1 is related to the number of cluster sensors which sending data to CH at the same time. The coefficient φ_2 is related to scanning the 'b' bit packet of data and loading it into memory.

The communication of neighbouring sensor nodes is enabled by a sensor radio. Radio energy dissipation model is shown in **Figure 8**.

The set of sensor nodes be denoted by $\mathbb{N}$. Each node i is assumed to generate data at a constant rate during its lifetime and the initial energy E_i. According to Ben Alla et al. and Shi et al. [24, 26], the energy consumption for transmitting L bits from node i to j can be determined as follows

$$E_{tx}(ij) = L * E_{elec} + L * E_{amp} * \left(d_{ij}\right)^{\propto} \quad (5)$$

and receive

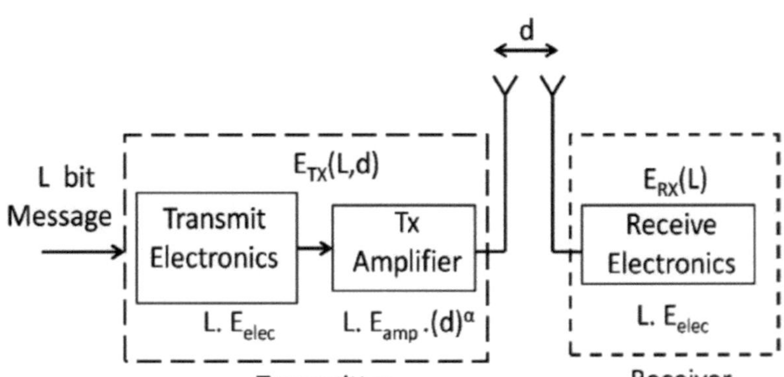

Figure 8. Radio energy dissipation model [24, 25].

$$E_{rx}(ij) = L * E_{elec} \tag{6}$$

where L = packet size, E_{elec} = energy dissipated to transmit or receive electronics, E_{amp} = energy dissipated by the power amplifier, $\alpha = 2$ for free-space fading and $\alpha = 4$ for multi-path fading, d = distance.

For evaluation we assume that each sensor node has the same transmission range. The neighbours of node i define as $N(ij) = \{j \in \mathbb{N} | (d(ij) \leq d)\}$

The transient energy can be defined by

$$E_{trans} = T_a * V[c_n * I_a + (1 - c_n) * I_{sl}], \tag{7}$$

where V = supply voltage, I_a and I_{sl} = current for active and sleeping mode, T_a == wake up duration.

If in the network are $N(i)$ sensor nodes, and have $C(j)$ clusters, then the total energy of sensor node in cluster of one information sending round can be expressed by equation [27],

$$E_N(ij) = \left[E_s + E_{log} + E_{tx}\left(d_{ij}\right) + E_{trans}\right], \tag{8}$$

and

$$E_{CH}(j) = \left[E_{s(CH)} + E_{log(CH)} + \left(\frac{N}{C} - 1\right)L * E_{elec} + E_{tx}\left(d_{ij}\right) + \frac{N}{C} * E_{rx} + E_{trans(CH)}\right] \tag{9}$$

The total energy consumed by the entire network is

$$E_{TN} = \sum_{j=1}^{C}\left(E_{CH}(j) + \sum_{i=1}^{N_j} E_N(ij)\right) \tag{10}$$

During data transfer phase, the nodes transmit messages to their cluster heads and the cluster heads transmit the aggregated messages to the sink. The data transfer energy consumed by a cluster head and node are defined by [26]

$$E_{CH|frame}(j) = \left[\left(\frac{N}{C} - m\right)L * E_{elec} + \left(\frac{N}{C} - m + 1\right)E_{tx|rx}\left(d_{ij}\right) + L \in \left(d_{ij}\right)^4\right], \tag{11}$$

$$E_{N|frame}(ij) = \left[L * E_{tx|rx}\left(d_{ij}\right) + L \in \left(d_{ij}\right)^2\right]. \tag{12}$$

There are C clusters and N nodes. In each iteration, m nodes are elected for each cluster. Thus, in each iteration $C*m$ nodes are elected as members of head-sets. The number of iterations required for all n nodes to be elected $\left(\frac{N}{C*m}\right)$ which is the number of iterations required in one round. Iteration consists of two phase: election and data transfer stage. Therefore the energy consumed in one iteration

$$E_{CH|iter} = E_{CH|elect} + E_{CH|data} \tag{13}$$

$$E_{N|iter} = E_{N|elect} + E_{N|data} \tag{14}$$

where energy consumptions in a data transfer stage are

$$E_{CH|data} = \omega_1 * DF * E_{CH|frame} \tag{15}$$

$$E_{N|data} = \omega_2 * DF * E_{N|frame} \tag{16}$$

$$\omega_1 = \left(\frac{1}{\frac{N}{C} - m + 1}\right) * \frac{1}{C} \tag{17}$$

$$\omega_2 = \left(\frac{\frac{N}{C} - m}{\frac{N}{C} - m + 1}\right) * \frac{1}{C} \tag{18}$$

The start energy E_{start} is the energy of a sensor node at the initial start time. This energy should be sufficient for at least one round. In one round, a node becomes a member of head-set for one time and a non-cluster head for $\left(\frac{N}{C * m} - 1\right)$t times. An estimation of E_{start} are used equation

$$E_{start} = \frac{E_{CH|elect} + E_{N|elect}}{C} + \frac{DF}{C} * \left(\omega_1 * E_{CH|frame} + \omega_2 * E_{N|frame}\right) \tag{19}$$

Our goal is minimizing the E_{TN} by using a dynamic clustering algorithm and dynamic cluster head selection algorithm, which is adaptive to the current MANET-IoT system conditions, analysing sensor nodes battery energy state and reduce their energy consumption.

Based on the location of the sink node (or base station), the optimal cluster numbers are applied to the two different locations that are both the centre of the sensing area and the outside of the sensing area. The optimal cluster number for the centre of the sensing area is given by [28, 29]

$$C_{opt} = \sqrt{N} \tag{20}$$

where N is the number of sensor nodes.

The optimal cluster number for the outside of the sensing area is given by

$$C_{opt} = \sqrt{N} * \frac{M}{\sqrt{M^2 + 6 * d_{sink}^{\ 2}}} \tag{21}$$

where N is the sensing area, d_{sink} is distance from the centre of sensing area to the outside location of the sink and M is the network diameter.

Optimization model has also been used to study maximum lifetime conditions for sensor networks. The model balances the competing minimum energy and maximum information objectives by limiting the minimum information to be extracted to the station and minimizing the energy required to do this. The objective function is to maximize the network lifetime of the given wireless sensor network configuration [30]

$$Z = \max\min\left\{f\left(\propto\left(\frac{E_{N,CH}}{E_{TN}}\right), \beta\left(\frac{T_{\gamma}}{T^{n}_{route}}\right), \delta\left(S_{ch,N}\right), \varepsilon\left(H_{route}\right)\right)\right\} \tag{22}$$

where $\propto$ is the coefficient of energy, β is the coefficient of lifetime, δ is the coefficient of signal strength and ε the is coefficient of route hops.

In general, we analysed an impact factor; therefore, sensor node parameters tied optimum logarithmic function:

$$f(\propto, \beta, \delta, \varepsilon) = \log\{\propto + \beta + \delta + \varepsilon\} \tag{23}$$

Because the optimum function will be transformed into a graph of weight function $G(x, y, z, \vartheta)$, Therefore, this function must be $G(x, y, z, \vartheta) > 0$, and $f(\propto, \beta, \delta, \varepsilon) > 0$. During the work that has been chosen continuous logarithmic function with the value for the application of the environment must be non-negative. The range of parameter is very different : energy consumed by the node E_{TN} is from 2 to 85%, T^{n}_{n} - = from 1 to T_{γ} of N, signal strength from –30 to –110 dBm, route hops from 1 to 16. For eliminating differences bound parameters and unifying their range have been consistently chosen to apply different parameter values for the calculation methods. The set Υ consisting of this coefficients and can be defined $\Upsilon = \{\propto, \beta, \delta, \varepsilon \in \mathbb{R}\}$. The function coefficient $\propto$ is converted to percentages, and restriction of this parameter is $\propto \in [0\ 1]$. Use the transform manipulation $\propto \rightarrow (1-x)^2$. Other parameters are: $\beta \in [1\ T^{n}_{n}]$, $\beta \rightarrow (0.15z)$, $\delta \in [0.027\ 0.85]$, $\delta \rightarrow (0.027y)^2$, $\varepsilon \in [1\ 16]$, $\varepsilon \rightarrow 0.1\vartheta$. According to the general definition of optimum function range, the common analytical function is given by

$$f(\propto, \beta, \delta, \varepsilon) = \log\left(\left(1-x\right)^2 + \left(0.027y\right)^2 + 0.15z + 0.1\vartheta\right) \tag{24}$$

The derived common analytical optimum function will be installing to the composite energy/lifetime efficient routing model. This function will be converted into the weight function, and this function will be used for calculations of sensor node values that are used in graph theory.

3.2. Proposed algorithm for data routing in the MANET-IoT system

In developing energy aware route selection schemes, we assume that WSN is a graph with vertices indicating sensor nodes and edges representing communication links between vertices. Graphs are a suitable model to describe complex networks, such as WSN. The weight on a vertex denotes residual energy of that node and the weight on an edge indicates the amount of energy that a node requires to transmit a unit of information along the edge [31]. The residual energy of a route is defined as the lowest energy level of any node on the route.

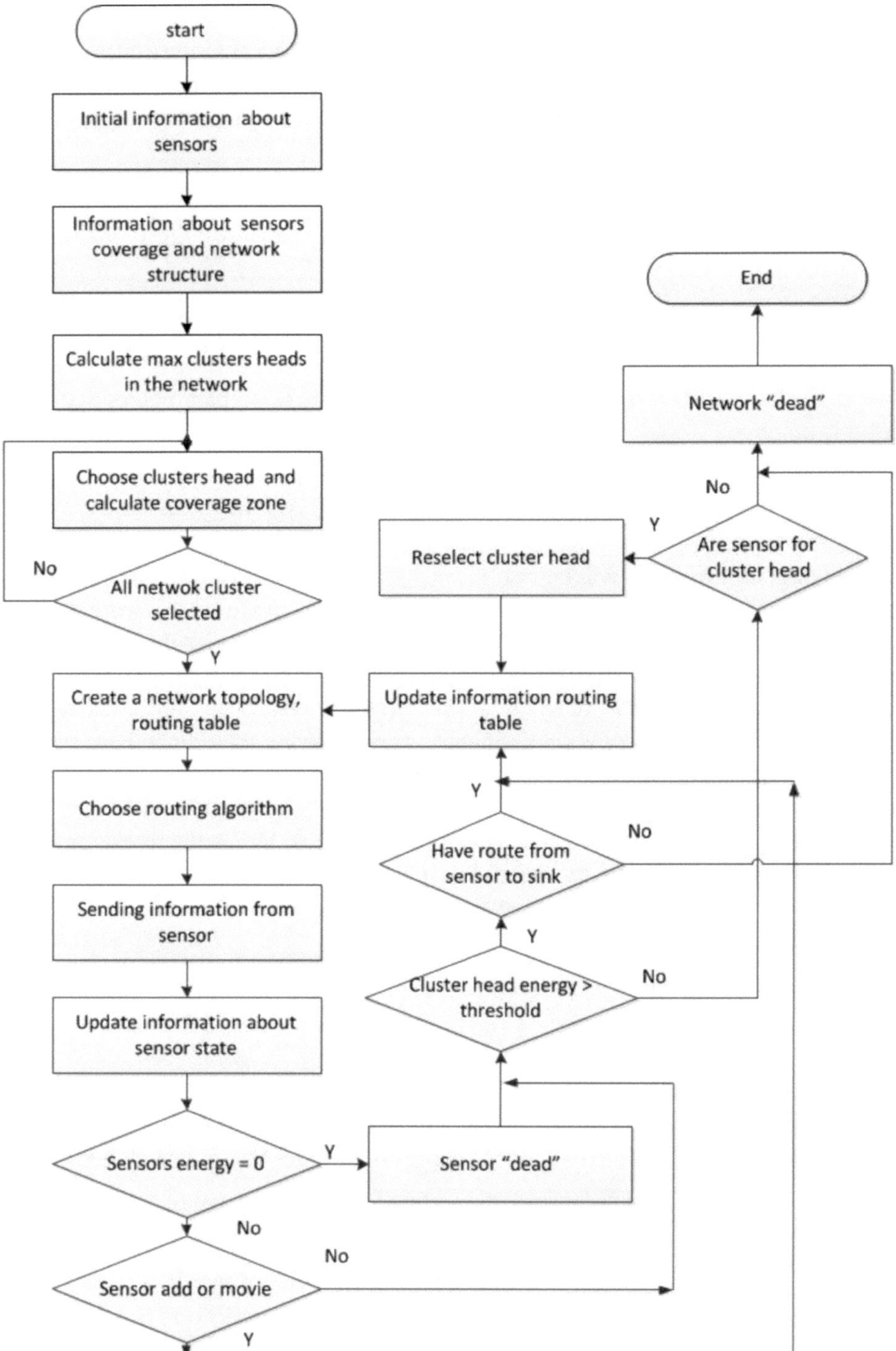

Figure 9. The flowchart of the proposed MANET-IoT system routing algorithm.

http://dx.doi.org/10.5772/66408

The energy consumed along a route is the sum of weights on all the edges present on the route. The most appropriate energy aware route selection scheme for WSNs is to utilize those nodes having higher energy levels and avoid those having lower energy levels, such that the overall energy consumption along the data forwarding path is minimized. For solution of this problem we composite routing over MANET-IoT networks using the combination of MANET and WSNs routing principles.

The proposed algorithm adopts a dynamical monitoring, with controls the energy of the cluster heads, and a predefined threshold value. The purpose of this monitoring mechanism is for transferring cluster head based on the comparison result between the energy of cluster head and threshold value.

The algorithm presented in **Figure 9** has three phases: setup, steady and threshold. First step is a cluster head selection. After the cluster head selection phase, all the selected cluster heads send an advertisement message to all the non-cluster head nodes in the field. Based on the received signal strength of the advertisement message, the non-cluster head nodes decide their cluster heads for the current round and send back a join request message to their selected cluster heads informing their membership which leads to the formation of cluster. The message sent to the cluster heads includes the node's ID as well as the location of the sender node.

When all the sensor nodes are deployed, the entire network starts to select the cluster heads and carry out clustering and layering. Then, the nodes begin to periodically collect data and transmit them to the sink node. With the change of time, the network topology structure is also changing. If cluster head energy is lower than the predefined threshold value, the

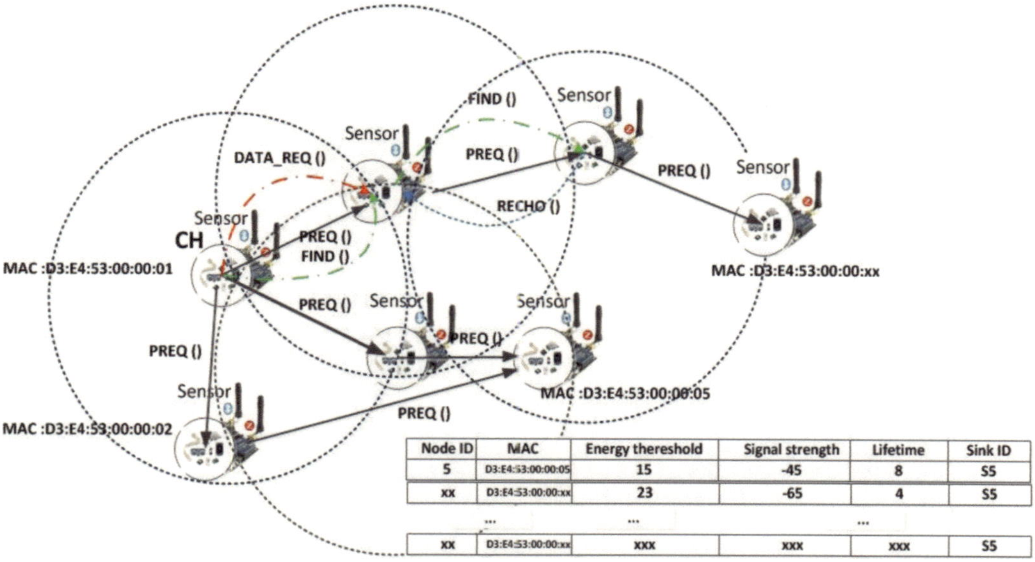

Node ID	MAC	Energy thereshold	Signal strength	Lifetime	Sink ID
5	D3:E4:53:00:00:05	15	-45	8	S5
xx	D3:E4:53:00:00:xx	23	-65	4	S5
	...	...		...	
xx	D3:E4:53:00:00:xx	xxx	xxx	xxx	S5

Figure 10. Messages exchange between nodes using the proposed algorithm.

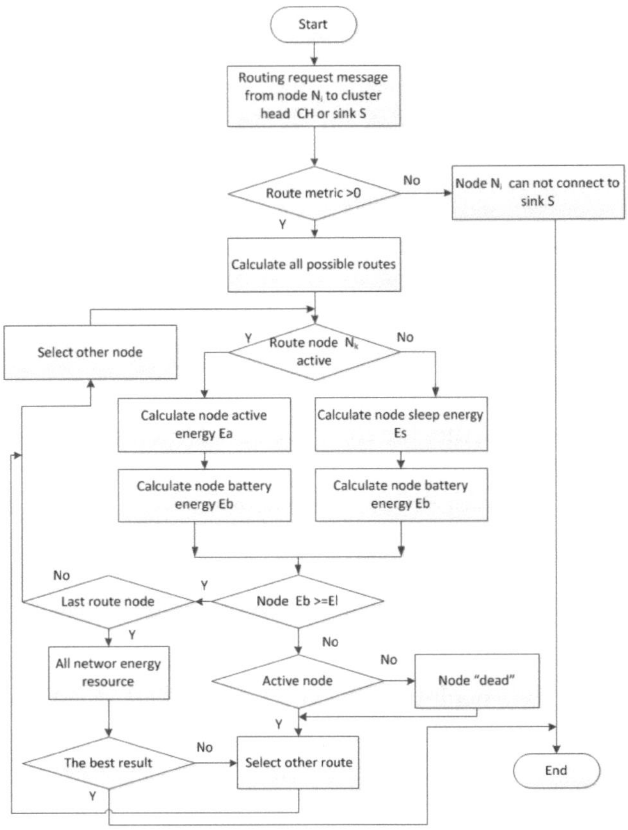

Figure 11. Proposed common route choosing algorithm.

`third loop is applied to replace cluster head by another node, which poses the largest energy within the cluster. The new cluster head continues to cooperate with cluster members. This way protects the cluster heads, which have lower energy. This mechanism can protect cluster heads from quick death and prolong the network lifetime. The messages exchanges between nodes are shown in **Figure 10**.

When have all information about network and nodes, then are choosing the routing method for transmission information. In this research work, our proposed common route choosing algorithm is presented in **Figure 11**. For evaluation network lifetime three route path selection methods are used: NP (node place), BST (node battery state) and ER (energy resource). The NP aim to find route with minimum hop and for searching nodes, node location parameters or methods are used (RSSI, AoA and ToA). The cluster head evaluates all neighbour nodes that are in the cluster. If the information does not satisfy required criterions, cluster heads send message for the neighbour cluster head to help find route to the sink. BST selects node which battery state is the higher. Using the ER method we calculate all network energy resource using the proposed algorithm. In the new algorithm, a threshold value is added in order to monitor the energy of node.

4. Performance evaluation of routing algorithms

Simulation experiments are carried out using Matlab (2010b). The principal goal of these simulations is to analyse our algorithm and compare it with other. For analysing and comparing the performance of our proposed method we used two metrics: node energy and network lifetime (or the number of rounds). Network lifetime is one of the main characteristics to evaluate the performance of sensor networks. Such a parameter includes coverage, connectivity and node availability. The network lifetime T_n^n is defined as that the sensor network loses connectivity. The route lifetime is defined as the first node fails, thus

$$T^n_{\text{route}} = \min T_\gamma,\ \gamma \in N \tag{25}$$

where T_γ is the lifetime of node γ in ij-route.

We test the proposed algorithm using an initial number of alive sensors $N = 17$, each with a range $d = 8$ m. We use a network of size $M = 20 \times 20$ m, with a sink located at point coordinates [$x = 7$, $y = 18$]. According our proposed solution, first we calculated the optimal number of cluster using Eq. (21). As shown in **Figure 12** that in our case the optimal number of clusters are 3.

The network at which we apply our tests is shown in **Figure 13**.

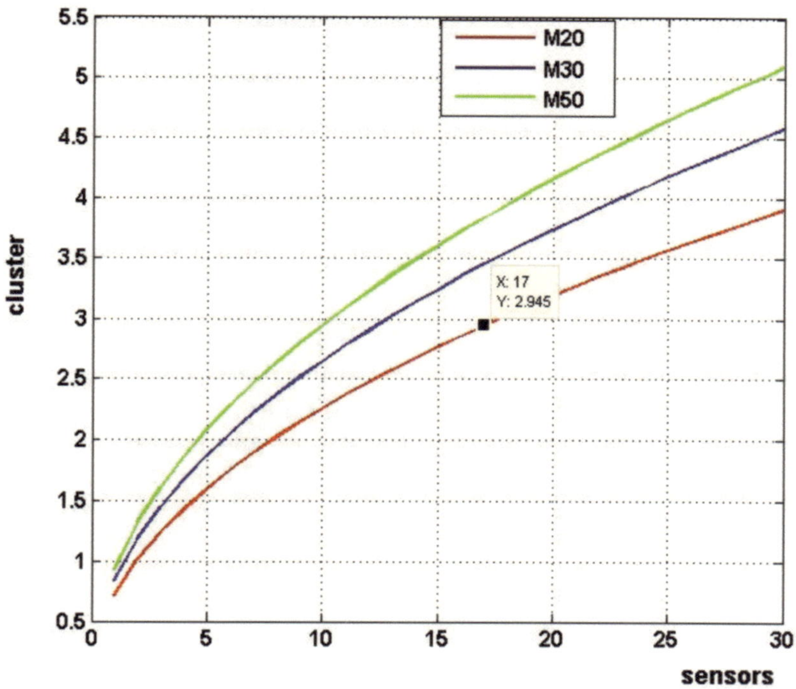

Figure 12. Optimum number of clusters versus sensors and network size.

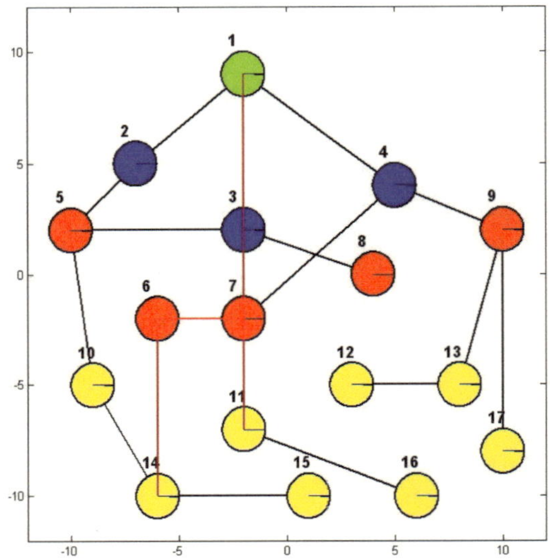

Figure 13. The test network structure.

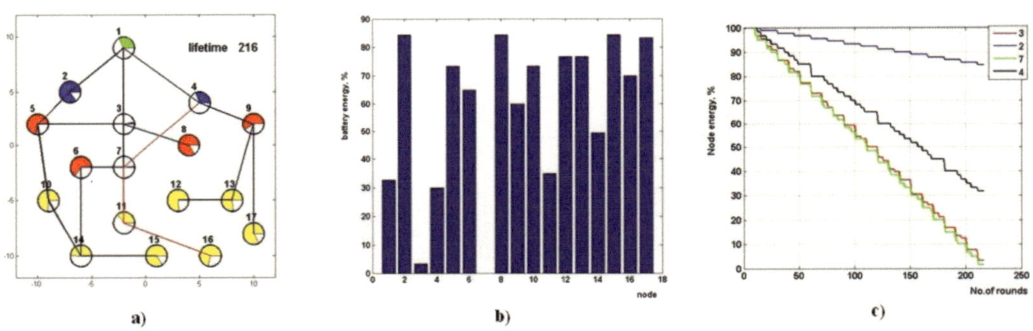

Figure 14. Simulation results (a) network lifetime, (b) each node battery energy, (c) dependency of node energy on the number of rounds.

Figure 13 shows the network topology structure. The green round circle denotes the sink. The blue round circle denotes the cluster heads. The red and yellow round circles denote the sensors, but red can be the cluster head also. The connection line denotes the path of a single hop from the sensor nodes to the cluster head. In the first scenario, sensors are sending information to the sink over three cluster heads. **Figure 14** presents the simulation results (a) network lifetime, (b) each node battery energy and (c) dependency of node energy on the number of rounds.

As can been seen in **Figure 14**, using such information to the routing method network lifetime (dimension is days) is 216, and the fastest losing power nodes 3 and 7. During the analysis of this data, we observe that the consumption of energy distribution is unbalanced in the network and observable the weakness network location. The next simulation step was to use routing change over the simulation period, when the node energy level is lower than the

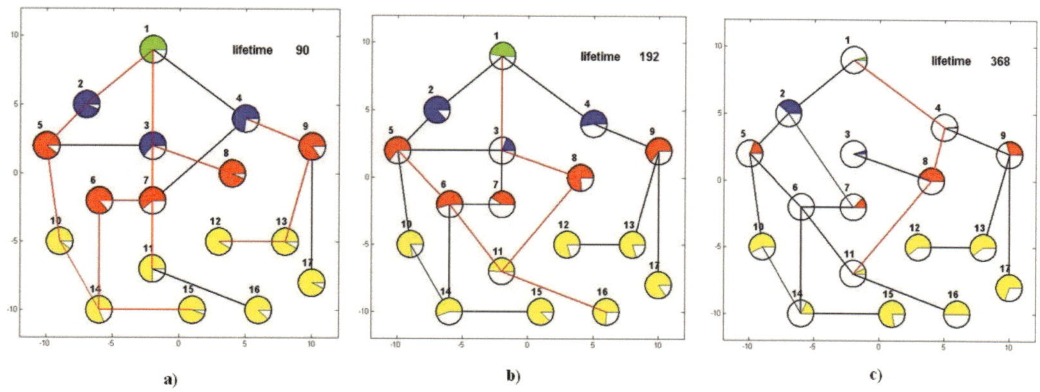

Figure 15. WSN lifetime using a node energy level threshold value for routing change.

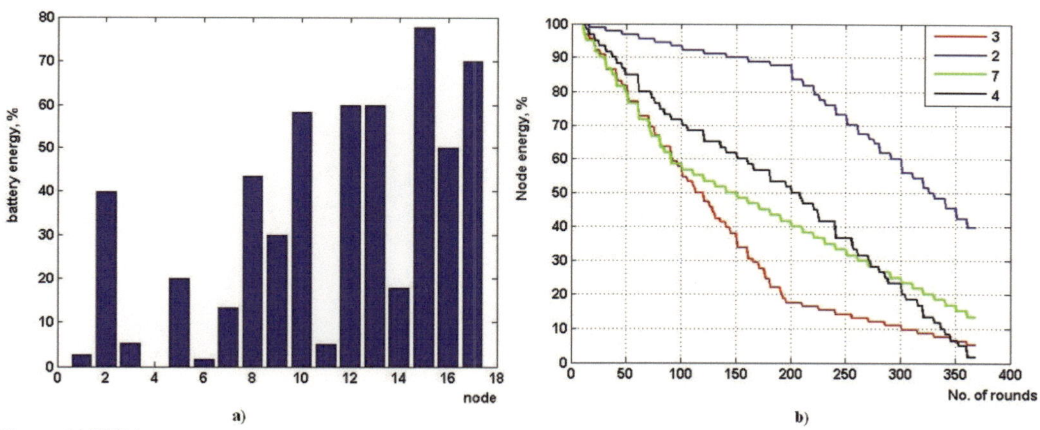

Figure 16. WSN energy parameters.

threshold value. **Figure 15** shows that after 90 rounds (a), the node 4 energy level is lower than the threshold value, therefore the sending information form node 7 we redirect from node 4 to node 3 and from nodes 11–7 to nodes 11–8. The next time (b) after 192 round we change other routes. Using this algorithm, our simulation network lifetime was 368 (c). The energy parameters are shown in **Figure 16**.

For evaluation of the effectives of our proposed algorithm, the next simulation was carried out. The simulation results are presented in **Figures 17** and **18**.

By comparing the results, we found that by using our proposed algorithm, the network lifetime is the longest than using simple or clustering without weight routing methods. The main objective of the dynamic cluster head rotation mechanism is to evenly distribute the energy load among all the sensor nodes so that there are no overly utilized sensor nodes that will run out of energy before the others. And we can see that the distribution of network nodes' energy consumption becomes smoother (**Figure 18**). The assumptions made for compare different routing are as follows: network nodes are homogeneous and not mobility; they are equipped

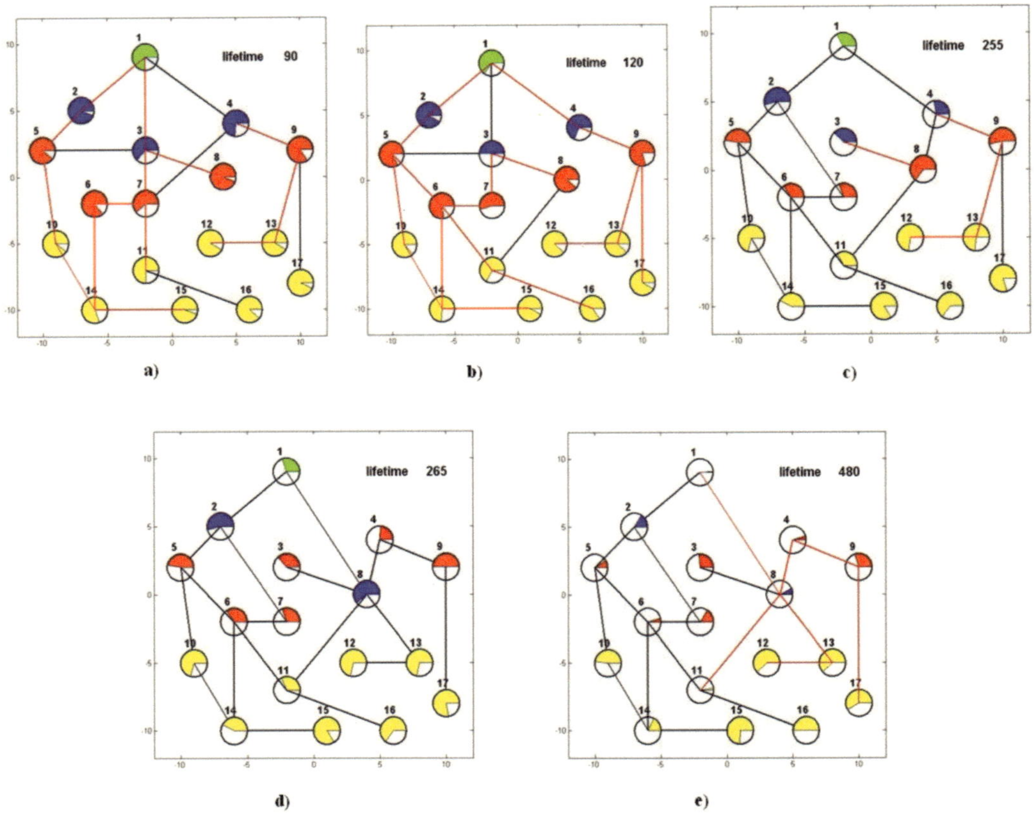

Figure 17. WSN lifetime using the proposed algorithm.

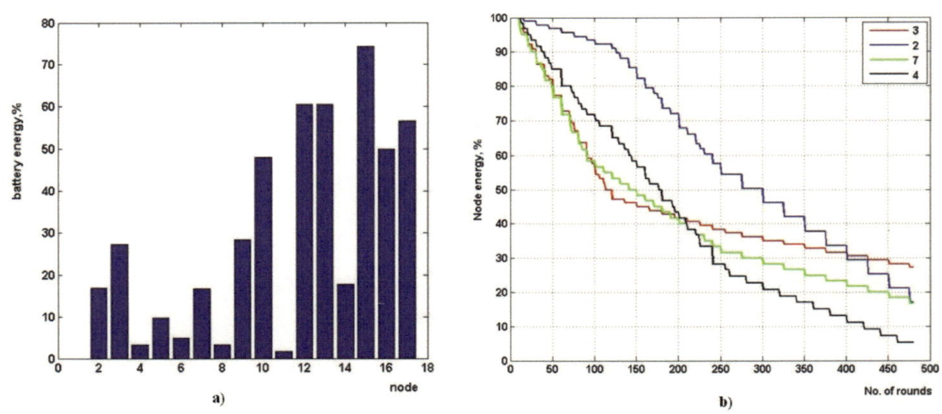

Figure 18. WSN energy parameters using the proposed algorithm.

with power control; have active and sleep mode; each sensor has a unique identifier and uniformly deployed over the target area to continuously monitor the environment.

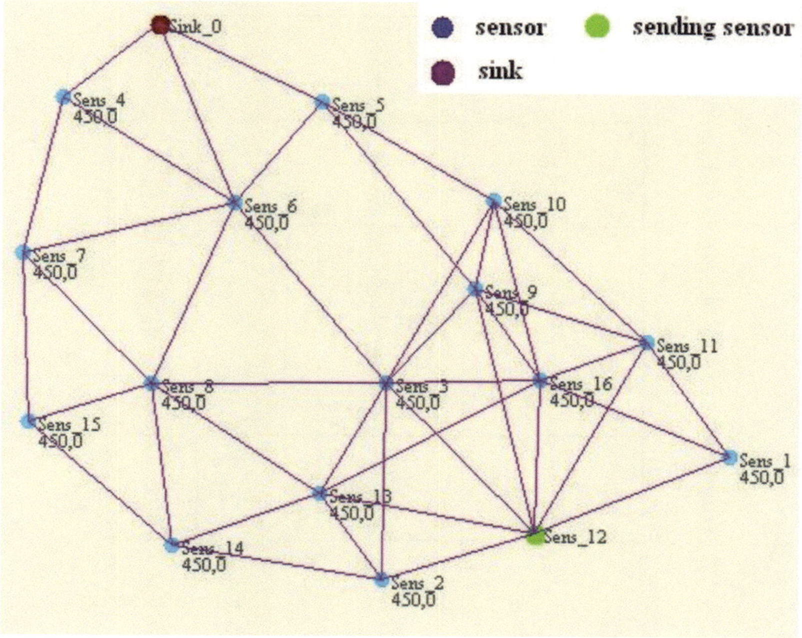

Figure 19. The simulation network topology.

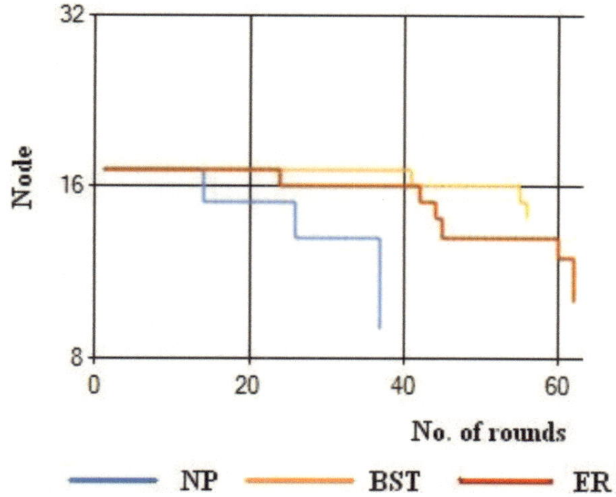

Figure 20. Network nodes' "dead" versus the number of rounds using three different routing algorithms.

The second simulations are conducted for evaluating effectiveness of the proposed algorithm ER compare with other two (node place (NP) and battery state (BST)). The network topology is presented in **Figure 19**.

After such a network simulation we have seen over time as changing the number of nodes on the network (**Figure 20**). The first network node falls out after 15 round using the BP method and using our proposed algorithm ER after 23 rounds. When using the BST method the first

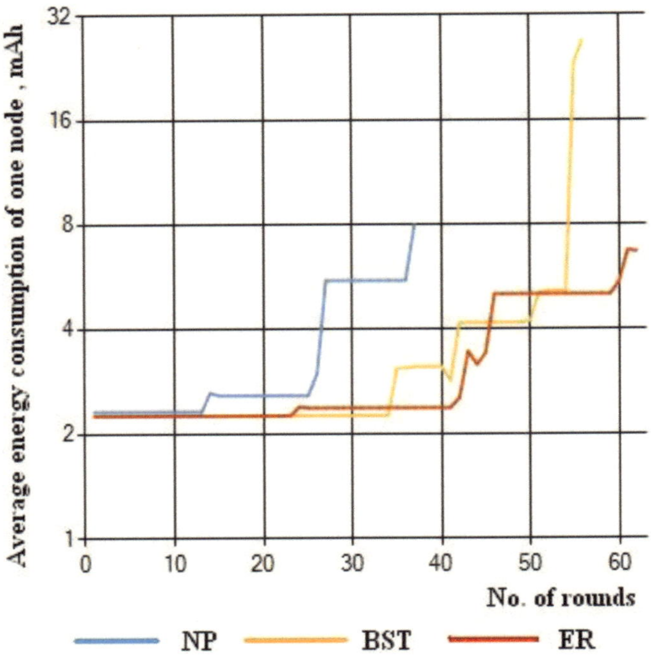

Figure 21. Average energy consumption of one node.

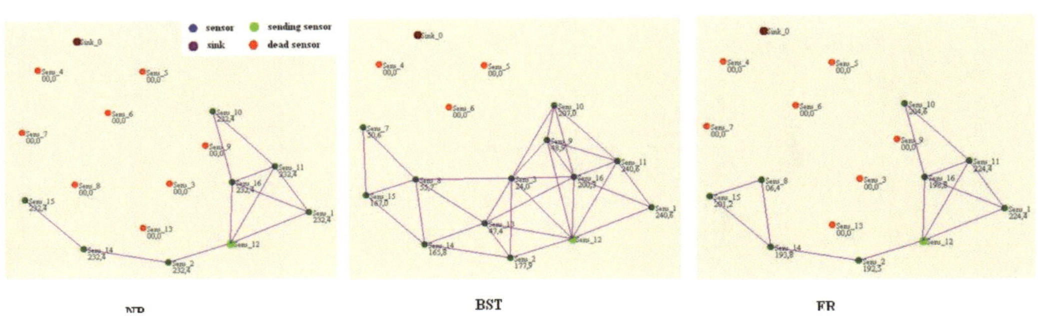

Figure 22. The network topology at the end of network lifetime.

node falls out from the network after 41, but then very suddenly battery energy of all nodes is ends. Network lifetimes of different methods are NP = 38, BST = 57 and ER = 63.

The average energy consumption of one node is shown in **Figure 21**, indicating the average energy at the time, which is utilized in the network for one node. Analysing this graph, we can see that the largest energy consumption is using the NP method. The BST method compared to the other two at the beginning of a lifetime of approximately constant amount of energy per one node is 32 rounds. Late using BST method of energy consumption per node sharply increases when the network nodes begin to leave one after the other. Such a sharp jump is because that the network nodes in more or less all the battery depletes a similar amount of energy and begins to fall out of the network, all one after the other. When the other two methods fall just in time for most working nodes through which passes the shortest route.

As we can see in **Figure 22** at the end of the network lifetime, there are nodes which energy is not zero and its can still be used in all three cases. It is an indicator of the best network energy resource utilization.

According simulation results, the NP and ER method network resource utilization is very similar. Using the BST routing method we can extend the time up to the first node falling out. This is important for the network when all sensors are the same and send the similar information.

5. Conclusion

In this chapter, we presented the proposed algorithm of energy efficient and safe-weighted clustering routing for the mobile IoT system using a combination of MANET and WSN routing principles. We choose the clustering method, because each sensor nodes in a network organize themselves into hierarchical structures. The simulation result show that if we use combination method for information routing in the wireless sensor network, we increase the lifetime of sensors in overall Internet of Things system. Because we used dynamical cluster head selection, the weighting factors are added for routing from the sensor to the sink. When the network is heterogeneous and mobility, the using routing weight is very important, because sensors have different characteristics, dynamical distance from the sink and CH node and if we want to choose the best route we need to calculate some objectives function. And this function must have possibility to eliminating differences bound parameters. For solving this we used the weight function, and this function will be used for calculations of each sensor node value and then calculation all route cost function.

Acknowledgement

This work was partially supported by the ICT COST Action IC1304—Autonomous Control for a Reliable Internet of Services (ACROSS), November 14, 2013—November 13, 2017, funded by European Union.

Author details

Rasa Bruzgiene*, Lina Narbutaite and Tomas Adomkus

*Address all correspondence to: rasa.bruzgiene@ktu.lt

Faculty of Informatics, Kaunas University of Technology, Kaunas, Lithuania

References

[1] ITU-T/Recommendation Y.2060. Overview of the Internet of Things [Internet]. 2012-06. Available from: http://www.itu.int/itu-t/recommendations/rec.aspx?rec=Y.2060 [Accessed: 2016-06-10]

[2] Aarti, S.S. Tyagi. Study of MANET: Characteristics, Challenges, Application and Security Attacks. International Journal of Advanced Research in Computer Science and Software Engineering. 2013;**3**(5):252–257.

[3] R. Balakrishna, Z. Hussain. A survey on Manets-Types, Characteristics, Applications and Protocols used. In: R. Balakrishna, L. Naveen, U.G. Nandish, editors. National Conference on Frontiers and Advances in Information Science and Technology FAIST13; 23–24 May, 2013;. Bangalore, India: RRCE; 2013.

[4] P. Nayak., R. Agrawal, S. Verma. Energy Aware Routing Scheme for Mobile Ad Hoc Network Using Variable Range Transmission. International Journal of Ad Hoc, Sensor & Ubiquitous Computing. 2012;**3**(4):53–63. DOI: 10.5121/ijasuc.2012.3406

[5] S. Agrawal, M. Lal Das. Internet of Things — A Paradigm Shift of Future Internet Applications. In: Nirma University International Conference on Engineering; 8–10 Dec, 2011; Ahmedabad, Gujarat: IEEE; 2011. pp. 1–7. DOI: 10.1109/NUiConE.2011.6153246

[6] O. Vermesan, P. Friess, editors. Internet of Things: Converging Technologies for Smart Environments and Integrated Ecosystems. 1st ed. Aalborg, Denmark: River Publishers; 2013. 364 p.

[7] P. Suresh., J. Vijay Daniel, V. Parthasarathy, R.H. Aswathy. A State of the Art Review on the Internet of Things (IoT) History, Technology and Fields of Deployment. In: International Conference on Science Engineering and Management Research (ICSEMR); 27–29 Nov, 2014; Chennai. IEEE; 2014. pp. 1–8. DOI: 10.1109/ICSEMR.2014.7043637

[8] D. Miorandi, S. Sicari, F. De Pellegrini, I. Chlamtac. Internet of Things: Vision, Applications and Research Challenges. Ad Hoc Networks. 2012;**10**(7):1497–1516. DOI: 10.1016/j.adhoc.2012.02.016

[9] J. Gubbia, R. Buyyab, S. Marusica, M. Palaniswamia. Internet of Things (IoT): A Vision, Architectural Elements, and Future Directions. Future Generation Computer Systems. 2013;**29**(7):1645–1660. DOI: 10.1016/j.future.2013.01.010

[10] P. Bellavista, G. Cardone, A. Corradi, L. Foschini. Convergence of MANET and WSN in IoT Urban Scenarios. IEEE Sensors Journal. 2013;**13**(10):3558-3567. DOI: 10.1109/JSEN.2013.2272099

[11] Gregory S. Yovanof., George N. Hazapis. An Architectural Framework and Enabling Wireless Technologies for Digital Cities & Intelligent Urban Environments. Wireless Personal Communications. 2009;**49**(3):445–463. DOI: 10.1007/s11277-009-9693-4

[12] N. Bessis, F. Xhafa, D. Varvarigou, R. Hill, M. Li, editors. Internet of Things and Inter-cooperative Computational Technologies for Collective Intelligence. 1st ed. Berlin: Springer-Verlag; 2013. 476 p. DOI: 10.1007/978-3-642-34952-2

[13] M. Potnuru, P. Ganti/University of Illinois Urbana-Champaign. Wireless Sensor Networks: Issues, Challenges and Survey of Solutions [Internet]. 2016. Available from: https://www.academia.edu/890321/Wireless_Sensor_Networks_Issues_Challenges_and_Survey_of_Solutions [Accessed: 02-06-2016]

[14] B. Bhuyan, H. Kumar Deva Sarma, N. Sarma, A. Kar, R. Mall. Quality of Service (QoS) Provisions in Wireless Sensor Networks and Related Challenges. Wireless Sensor Network. 2010;**2**:861–868. DOI: 10.4236/wsn.2010.211104

[15] M. Rath, U.P. Rout. Analysis and Study of Security Aspect and Application Related Issues at the junction of MANET and IoT. International Journal of Research in Engineering and Technology. 2015;**4**(13):426–430.

[16] A. Boukerche, B. Turgut, N. Aydin, M.Z. Ahmad, L. Bölöni, D. Turgut. Routing Protocols in Ad Hoc Networks: A Survey. Computer Networks. 2011;**55**(13):3032–3080. DOI: 10.1016/j.comnet.2011.05.010

[17] L. Hanzo, R. Tafazolli. A Survey of QoS Routing Solutions for Mobile Ad hoc Networks. IEEE Communications Surveys & Tutorials. 2007;**9**(2):50–70. DOI: 10.1109/COMST.2007.382407

[18] K. Akkaya, M. Younis. A Survey on Routing Protocols for Wireless Sensor Networks. Ad Hoc Networks. 2005;**3**(3):325–346. DOI: 10.1016/j.adhoc.2003.09.010

[19] Y. Tian, R. Hou. An Improved AOMDV Routing Protocol for Internet of Things. In: International Conference on Computational Intelligence and Software Engineering (CiSE); 10–12 Dec. 2010; Wuhan. IEEE; 2010. pp. 1–4. DOI: 10.1109/CISE.2010.5676940

[20] T. Tsvetkov. RPL: IPv6 Routing Protocol for Low Power and Lossy Networks. In: Network Architectures and Services; July 2011. pp. 59–66. DOI: 10.2313/NET-2011-07-1_09

[21] X. Wang, editor. Mobile Ad-Hoc Networks: Protocol Design. InTech. Rijeka, Croatia. 2011; 666 p.

[22] R. Tandon. Determination of Optimal Number of Clusters in Wireless Sensor Networks. International Journal of Computer Networks & Communications (IJCNC). 2012;**4**:235–249. DOI: 10.5121/ijcnc.2012.4415

[23] M.A. Matin, editor. Wireless Sensor Networks – Technology and Applications. InTech. Rijeka, Croatia. 2012; 386 p. DOI: doi.org/10.5772/1100

[24] S. Ben Alla, A. Ezzati, A. Mohsen. Hierarchical Adaptive Balanced Routing Protocol for Energy Efficiency in Heterogeneous Wireless Sensor Networks. In: Energy Efficiency – The Innovative Ways for Smart Energy, the Future Towards Modern Utilities. InTech; Rijeka, Croatia. pp. 313–336. DOI: doi.org/10.5772/47789

[25] S. Hussain, A.W. Matin. Energy Efficient Hierarchical Cluster-Based Routing for Wireless Sensor Networks [thesis]. Jodrey School of Computer Science Acadia University Wolfville, Nova Scotia, Canada; 2005; 33 p.

[26] J. Shi, A. Calveras, Y. Cheng, K. Liu. A Novel Power Efficient Location-Based Cooperative Routing with Transmission Power-Upper-Limit for Wireless Sensor Networks. Sensors. 2013;**13**:6448–6476. DOI: 10.3390/s130506448

[27] I. Butun, I-H. Ra, R. Sankar. An Intrusion Detection System Based on Multi-Level Clustering for Hierarchical Wireless Sensor Networks. Sensors. 2015;**15**:28960–28978. DOI: 10.3390/s151128960

[28] P.K. Panda. Study of Energy and Trust Aware Cluster Head Selection for Real Time Wireless Sensor Network [thesis]. Jadavpur University, KolkataWest Bengal, India; 2013. 71 p.

[29] M. Ali Shah, G. Abbas, A.B. Dogar, Z. Halim. Scaling Hierarchical Clustering and Energy Aware Routing for Sensor Networks. Complex Adapt System Model. Berlin: Springer Berlin Heidelberg; 2015. 23 p. DOI: 10.1186/s40294-015-0011-6

[30] M.A. Razzaque, S. Dobson. Energy-Efficient Sensing in Wireless Sensor Networks Using Compressed Sensing. Sensors. 2014;**14**:2822–2859. DOI: 10.3390/s140202822

[31] T-J. Chan, C.-M. Chen, Y-F. Huang, J-Y. Lin, T-R. Chen. Optimal Cluster Number Selection in Ad-hoc Wireless Sensor Networks. WSEAS transactions on Communications. 2008;**7**(8):837–846.

Chapter 6

Radio Frequency-Based Indoor Localization in Ad-Hoc Networks

Mehdi Golestanian, Joshua Siva and
Christian Poellabauer

Additional information is available at the end of the chapter

http://dx.doi.org/10.5772/66523

Abstract

The increasing importance of location-aware computing and context-dependent information has led to a growing interest in low-cost indoor positioning with submeter accuracy. Localization algorithms can be classified into range-based and range-free techniques. Additionally, localization algorithms are heavily influenced by the technology and network architecture utilized. Availability, cost, reliability and accuracy of localization are the most important parameters when selecting a localization method. In this chapter, we introduce basic localization techniques, discuss how they are implemented with radio frequency devices and then characterize the localization techniques based on the network architecture, utilized technologies and application of localization. We then investigate and address localization in indoor environments where the absence of global positioning system (GPS) and the presence of unique radio propagation properties make this problem one of the most challenging topics of localization in wireless networks. In particular, we study and review the previous work for indoor localization based on radio frequency (RF) signaling (like Bluetooth-based localization) to illustrate localization challenges and how some of them can be overcome.

Keywords: ad-hoc networks, wireless sensor networks (WSNs), localization, radio frequency (RF) signaling, Bluetooth low energy (BLE), Wi-Fi, XBee, indoor localization, range-based localization

1. Introduction

Localization is a key requirement of most mobile and wireless networks. For example, wireless sensor networks are often deployed in an ad-hoc fashion, which means that the locations of the sensors are not known a priori [1]. Localization is necessary to provide a physical context to sensor readings for services such as intrusion detection, inventory and supply chain management. It is also a fundamental task for sensor network services such as geographic routing and coverage area management [1, 2]. Over the last few decades, localization technologies have undergone significant progress and they now play a crucial role for many location- and context-aware services and applications such as navigation, robotics, patient monitoring and emergency response systems.

Localization algorithms can be classified into either range-based or range-free. Range-based localization (like GPS and some forms of cellular-based positioning) can have very high accuracy by taking measurements of a signal at the cost of computational and implementation complexity. In contrast, range-free localization algorithms (such as simple cell-based localization) can provide a less accurate position (but perhaps "good enough" for the specific purpose) with a much more simple implementation. Additionally, the physical environment can have a great impact on the performance of a chosen localization algorithm. For example, while global positioning system (GPS) has been the primary localization approach for outdoor environments, indoor environments (and all other GPS-denied areas) face severe challenges such as the limited accuracy of techniques like cellular-based positioning [2] and radio propagation characteristics that can differ significantly from outdoor environments [3]. Therefore, as one of the most challenging topics in localization, indoor localization has attracted the attention of many researchers both in industry and academia.

In recent years, a variety of novel approaches have been presented, including positioning based on FM signaling [4], Wi-Fi trilateration [5] and low energy Bluetooth beaconing (e.g., iBeacons) [6]. Most such techniques rely on the received signal strength indicator (RSSI) as the main parameter to extract distance information with acceptable accuracy [7]. Infrared-based indoor localization [8], signal fingerprint-based localization [9] and image-based indoor localization [10] are examples of localization that do not rely on RSSI or other similar signal or link measurement for distance determination. However, these methods typically introduce higher costs and complexity and may not be as readily available.

Availability, cost, reliability and accuracy of localization are the most important parameters when selecting a localization method and technology. Among existing technologies, RF-based methods based on Bluetooth and Bluetooth low energy (BLE), Wi-Fi and XBee are popular choices due to their availability (e.g., BLE is available on most modern smart devices), low power consumption (particularly BLE and XBee) and low cost. Although RF-based methods have several advantages for localization purposes, they also have a significant shortcoming in indoor environments, i.e., prior work has shown that RSSI is not a reliable metric and that it can easily be affected by the unique characteristics of the indoor environment [11]. On the other hand, timing-based ranging approaches have attracted much attention using technologies such as XBee/ZigBee [12], ultra wideband (UWB) [13] and Wi-Fi [14]. Timing methods come with their own collection of advantages and disadvantages in an ad-hoc and indoor environment. In this chapter, we investigate recent work involving in the field of RF-based localization to address the challenges of RSSI- and timing-based localization in indoor environments and then review approaches that can be used to address these challenges.

The structure of the chapter is organized as follows: Section 2 presents the basic concepts of localization and its application including a discussion of common characteristics of localization algorithms. Section 3 narrows down the localization problem to indoor localization algorithms based on RF signaling. Section 4 discusses some of the challenges associated with RF-based indoor localization. Section 5 reviews how some of these challenges are addressed in recent work and addresses future research directions to tackle the remaining challenges.

2. Introduction to localization

2.1. Overview

Before we investigate localization in an indoor environment with radio frequency devices in detail, we must first establish a solid understanding of localization. The general problem of localization is the determination of the position of an object (or person) within a specific space. This location could be within some local coordinate system or it could be a global coordinate system, such as latitude and longitude coordinates on the Earth's surface. The best-known solution to the localization problem is the global positioning system (GPS), which uses the time of arrival of signals from multiple satellites to determine where the GPS receiver is located within several meters. Moreover, companies such as Apple, Microsoft, Google and Skyhook all have methods of estimating a user's location by fusing GPS, Wi-Fi and cellular data for a multitude of purposes ranging from enabling context-aware applications to locating stolen devices. The usefulness and importance of localization are difficult to understate as is the difficulty and multitude of approaches to solving this problem. Not all localization systems are created equal, for they are implemented using a variety of technologies according to the necessities of the system in which the location is required. For example, locating a car on the road has different requirements than locating a person in a shopping mall or a drone in a building. Based on these requirements, such as high accuracy or low power consumption, a localization system can be developed either by repurposing or piggybacking on existing technology or by using an existing localization system, namely, GPS.

A common way that localization is implemented is to determine the distances between a target and a sufficient number of reference points. This process is referred to as ranging. Once these distances are known, then it is possible to approximate the location of the target geometrically through trilateration or min-max. Trilateration works by using the measured distance as the radius of a circle around a reference point. The intersection of three circles is the estimated location of the target. If the circles do not intersect at a single point then further action must be taken to improve the estimate. An example of trilateration in two dimensions is shown in **Figure 1**. The min-max method takes the measured distance between the target and the reference point and uses it to form a square with side length twice that distance with the reference point that made the measurement at the center. The target is assumed to be in the center of the rectangle formed by the intersecting reference nodes' squares. An example of min-max in two dimensions is shown in **Figure 2**. Methods of localization using trilateration or min-max belong to the group of range-based localization methods. Because they are based on geometry and they are, perhaps, the most straightforward localization algorithms and have the potential for providing highly accurate location estimates.

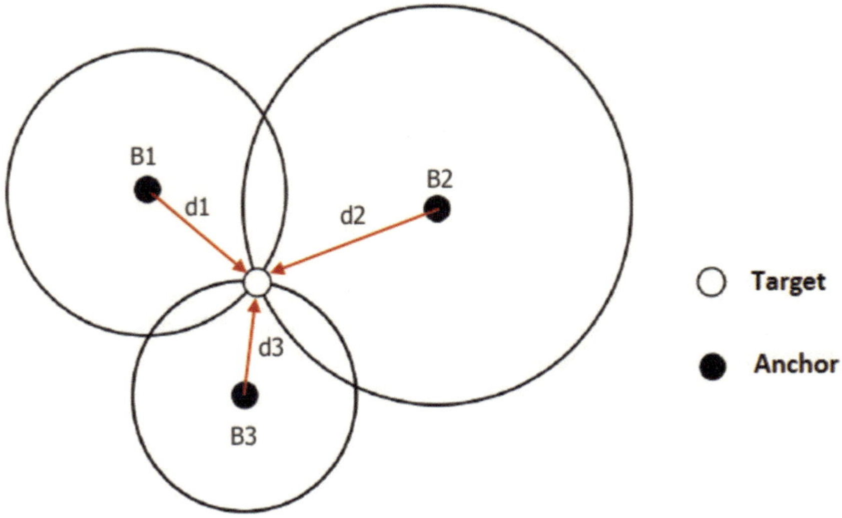

Figure 1. Trilateration technique with three reference points.

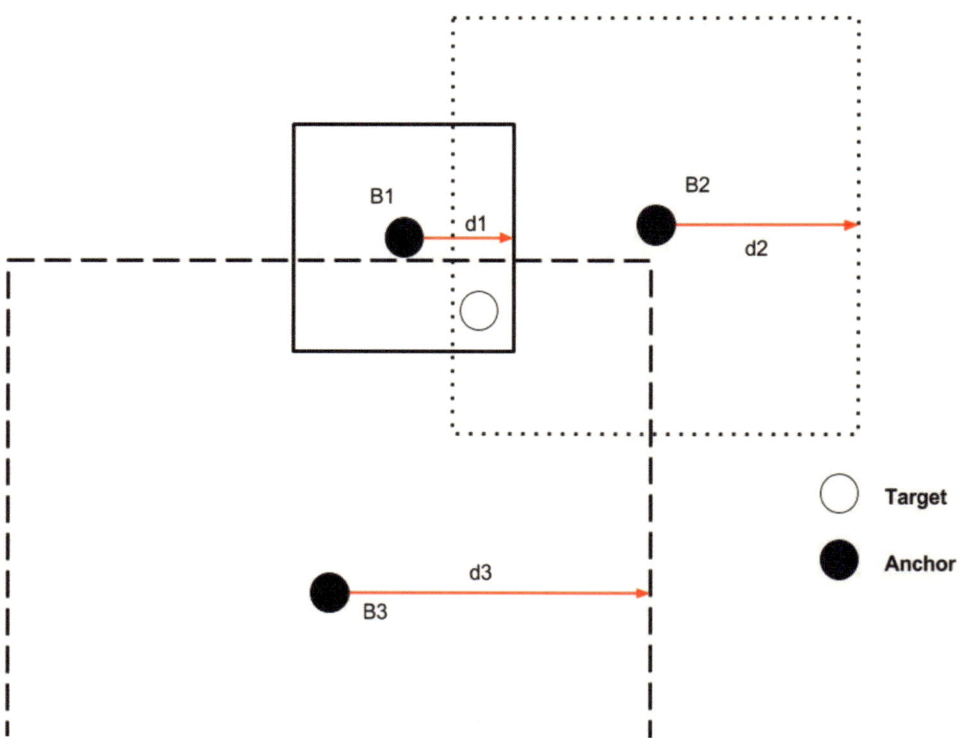

Figure 2. Min-max technique with three reference points.

GPS is an example of such a system, because once the time of flight (ToF) of the signals from the GPS satellites to the GPS receiver is known, then it is simply a matter of multiplying the speed of the signal (the speed of light) by the time it took to travel from the satellites to the receiver (accounting for relativistic effects along the way). Note that this relies on the sender and receiver having synchronized clocks to determine the time of arrival (ToA). Time-based ranging can also be accomplished through what is called time difference of arrival (TDoA). In this method, one needs to only measure the difference in arrival time between two signals with different (known) propagation speeds. For example, one could measure the arrival time of a radio signal and that of an auditory signal and because the speed of the signals is known, it would be a simple matter to determine the distance to the target which initiated both signals. The final method of ranging relies on measuring the amount that a signal decays as it travels from (or to) a known location. That is, if we know how a signal such as a sound or a radio wave diminishes as it travels and we also know the strength of the signal to begin with, then we can determine how far the signal traveled by measuring its strength at the receiver.

It is not always necessary to determine the distance between some reference points and a target. Methods of localization that estimate a location without using ranges are called range-free. This class of localization algorithm is characterized by its use of network connectivity and geometry as well as radio characteristics to estimate the location of a target node. For example, given three anchor nodes (nodes whose locations are known) and a target that has a connection with all of them allow us to estimate the target's location by finding the centroid of the triangle created by the three anchors. There are many methods that improve this simple "find the centroid" approach as well as other methods that estimate distances based on the known anchor positions and the connectivity of the network. In general, range-based localization methods are characterized by fairly high accuracy at the cost of higher computational complexity compared to range-free localization. Additionally, some ranging methods, such as those based on timing, may require hardware that devices in a resource-constrained sensor network may not have.

Localization in an ad-hoc network further complicates the localization process by placing stronger constraints on the resources available and how they are accessed. Ad-hoc networks, whether they are mobile ad-hoc networks (MANETs), vehicular ad-hoc networks (VANETs), or wireless sensor networks (WSNs), impose some limit on the amount of information available at any particular node and come with the added complication of having to share that data in an ad-hoc manner with other nodes in the network. For localization purposes, this means that combining widespread sources of information to estimate a range or location may no longer be possible. In fact, it may not even be possible to estimate an absolute location if the network does not include any anchors. Additionally, adding in the issue of mobility, whether it is the somewhat predictable mobility of a VANET or the less predictable movement of nodes in a MANET, turns the localization problem into a tracking problem and also needs to be balanced with how and where localization computations are going to be carried out in the network.

2.2. Characteristics of localization algorithms

Aside from the primary classification as a range-based or range-free, which is largely dictated by the hardware employed, localization systems can be further distinguished by their various characteristics including their network topology, computational strategy, use of anchors and ability to handle mobility, whether it be the anchors or the targets that are mobile.

The network topology is closely associated with the method of computation and has a major impact on the localization methods available because it dictates how information is going to be passed and to whom it will be passed. For example, in a star topology, the end nodes will not be able to communicate directly (or at all) with neighboring end nodes, which means that timing-based approaches may be difficult to implement and computation will need to be carried out at the master node. However, if a mesh topology is available, then there are few restrictions (imposed by the network) on the method of localization and it opens the door to distributed computation and cooperative localization.

The availability of anchors can be a hardware constraint if a global reference frame is in use and GPS is unavailable. Anchors can also take the form of a node with a known location in an arbitrary (but consistent) frame of reference, so lacking even these data are also a possibility. The availability of an anchor could be determined by the nodes' mobility and location; for example, a node moving about within a building may become an anchor when it is in a location where it can receive a GPS signal. Anchor-based localization algorithms are those that *require* anchors to function, whereas anchor-free algorithms could operate in their absence. Range-free localization algorithms that rely on finding the centroid of the shape formed by a set of nodes can only function if the locations of the nodes are known. In contrast, the range-based localization (e.g., ToF) can localize targets without anchors.

The various forms of mobility (or lack thereof) that a localization algorithm can handle are a characteristic that may be imposed by the hardware on the nodes or it may simply be an assumption made by the designers. For example, the computational burden than can be handled by sensors in a WSN may be severely limited, so the design of an algorithm that can handle precise tracking on such hardware would be infeasible. Similarly, the algorithm designers may assume that the targets to be localized are generally static or that their movements are fairly predictable.

In addition to these characteristics, considerations must be made regarding the impact of the localization algorithm on the normal network communication and the environment in which a localization system is to be deployed. The former consideration is one that is more important with regard to optimization, so it will not be discussed here. The latter is a point that will be considered in the next section as we discuss radio frequency (RF)-based localization with a focus on its implementation indoors and the challenges arising from that.

3. RF-based indoor localization

3.1. Radio frequency devices

The radio frequency devices under consideration in this chapter are Wi-Fi, Bluetooth/BLE and XBee devices due to their wide commercial availability and frequent use in ad-hoc networks. Wi-Fi is a well-known and ubiquitous radio technology based on the IEEE 802.11 standard. It operates in the 2.4 and 5 GHz bands with three nonoverlapping channels in the former and two dozen in the latter. Bluetooth falls under the IEEE 802.15.1 standard, operates in the 2.4 GHz band and is designed for wireless communication over short ranges. Instead of focusing on replacing wired networks, Bluetooth has found great usefulness in enabling communication on a smaller scale. BLE is a version of Bluetooth aimed at reducing power consumption, which has made it possible to integrate Bluetooth into power-constrained devices. BLE has also led to the development of Bluetooth beacons, which can be used for proximity detection for the purposes of driving context-aware applications such as navigation or advertisements in shopping malls. Finally, there are XBee radios that are designed for low data rate communication in personal area networks. They also operate in the 2.4 GHz band, have low bandwidth and are widely used for home automation and Internet of Things (IoT) applications. Since all of these forms of radios operate in similar frequency bands, they can and will interfere with each other; moreover, they all experience similar behavior with respect to radio wave propagation. With this in mind, there are a variety of range-based and range-free localization methods that can be implemented with all of these radios; however, there are some methods that may be better suited to one radio than another.

3.2. Range-based localization

As introduced above, range-based localization methods are used for triangulation, trilateration, or min-max. The go-to method of ranging, due to its simplicity, is RSS ranging, which relies on the notion that the strength of a radio signal decays in a reliable and easily calculable way. One common approach is to assume that the antenna is isotropic and then make use of a path loss model to solve for the distance given the power of the signal at the source and at some unknown point. Other approaches include developing different path loss models as in Refs. [15, 16] and improving the estimated distances or locations through the use of maximum-likelihood estimation [17] or a Kalman filter [18]. Almost all of these methods of RSS ranging involve some sort of calibration (solving for environmental characterization values, calculating a path loss model, etc.) to be effective.

Another common form of ranging is to calculate the ToF of the radio signal from the sender to the receiver. Since the speed of the radio signal is the speed of light, the distance can be calculated readily. The difficulty lies in how to precisely measure ToF because the processing delay between the arrival of the signal at the radio and when these data are read at the application layer is significant and can greatly overshadow the actual signal propagation time. Rather than perform one-way ranging (OWR), where both nodes must have clocks that are synchronized, another method is to perform two-way ranging (TWR), where a message in not only sent from one node to the other, but the other node also responds with an acknowledgment. TWR is helpful because it helps to account for the processing times on either end and also does not require that the two have synchronized clocks. One can go even further and perform symmetric double-sided TWR (SDS-TWR) in which the TWR procedure is run through twice starting once at each node. This method can help with issues such as clock drift [19], which are not addressed by TWR. A final method of ToF ranging (described in Ref. [14]) leverages the ability to analyze channel characteristics combined with communication across many channels to determine ToF. The key to this method is to change finding the ToF into an application of the Chinese Remainder Theorem by analyzing the phase of the arriving signal across many channels of communication. One drawback of this last method is that it requires both the hardware and software to support such an analysis of the arriving signal, which may not be the case for a lot of consumer radio products.

The final method of radio frequency ranging is ranging in the general sense of measuring something between a reference node and a target node. Determining the angle of arrival (AoA) is a ranging method in which the angle between a reference node and an unknown node in the former's frame of reference is determined. There are two ways that this has been accomplished in the literature. The first method is to use an antenna array so that the time difference of arrival at each of the antennas in the array of the signal can be used to calculate the AoA of the signal. The second approach is referred to as synthetic aperture radar (SAR) and entails moving an antenna at a predetermined speed in a predetermined direction (for example, rotation about an axis). Using the time difference of arrival at the antenna at different points in its trajectory, the direction of the signal can be determined. With additional sensors that can account for the movement of the node, SAR can be accomplished across an unknown trajectory as well as mentioned in Ref. [20].

3.3. Range-free localization

The accuracy of range-free localization methods is typically less than that of the range-based methods; however, these methods have the advantage of simplified implementation and hardware requirements. Additionally, it is not always necessary to calculate an exact location, so range-free localization displays varying levels of accuracy and complexity, so that the right tool can be chosen for the job.

One of the most accurate forms of range-free localization is called fingerprinting and relies on RSS measurements to develop a radio map of a location. Rather than attempt to draw a relationship between the RSS measurements and the distance between the unknown and known nodes, the RSS measurements at many known locations are stored in a database during a configuration phase. Later, a new node that enters the mapped area can get its location by having its signal strength readings compared against the database.

There are many methods that revolve around the use of network connectivity information in addition to the known location of a set of nodes. With this information, the centroid of the triangle formed by three nodes with known locations is used as the location estimate of a node to which all three are connected. There are a variety of implementations of the centroid method that differ, largely, by the geometry they wish to exploit. Another method of localization, which can be used in a multihop network, is DV-Hop, or distance vector hop [21], range-free localization. This method piggybacks on the distance vector routing algorithm with the knowledge of some of the node locations to estimate the length of a hop. The hop length estimate is then used to estimate the distances from the nodes with known locations to the target nodes. The final method of range-free localization addressed here is a simple proximity-based localization system in which connectivity to a reference node is assumed to mean that the target is located in the same place. If the signal range of the reference node can be controlled, then this method can be useful for room-level localization.

4. Challenges of RF-based indoor localization

4.1. Evaluation parameters

In order to study the challenges of the localization methods and evaluate their performance, we first need to present some metrics and concepts, which define their constraints and limitations.

(i) Localization accuracy: The localization accuracy is one of the most crucial parameters depending on the application of localization. For example, in safety applications in vehicular environments for pedestrian protection from accidents, the highest localization accuracy is desired (submeter accuracy). For less sensitive applications, lower accuracy coarse ranging (i.e., immediate, near and far region) is acceptable and for GPS-based localization, an accuracy of a few meters can be sufficient. The localization strategy, network structure, number of beacons and the devices' capabilities and technologies are other parameters that can impact the localization accuracy.

(ii) Localization reliability: Another important aspect of localization algorithms is the reliability of the methods, i.e., how consistent a localization method can be in different situations. Environment, the mobility of devices and objects in the network and type of technology are a few aspects that can impact the reliability of the localization method. Specifically, in RF-based localization based on analysis of RSSI to extract proximity information, the susceptibility of RSSI to multipath and shadowing caused by environmental changes is the main challenge to reliability (and accuracy). We will explore this further in the next section.

(iii) Power requirements: Networks (especially sensor networks) can have strict power requirements, which can impact localization performance. Two clear ways that power requirements impact localization are in the computational complexity of the localization algorithm chosen and the communication technology utilized. In the latter case, strict power requirements may push one to consider using BLE or XBee rather than Wi-Fi.

(iv) Availability/cost: For practical implementations of localization algorithms, cost and availability of the technologies and devices are the two essential factors. For example, BLE is one of the most popular and available technologies in smart devices and can easily be used for many localization purposes.

4.2. Challenges

One of the main shortcomings of RSSI-based localization (such as Bluetooth-based localization) in indoor environments is that RSSI measurements only provide a rough estimate of the distance between a transmitter and a receiver. In realistic environments, increasing the distance between the transmitter and the receiver does not necessarily decrease the signal strength (especially indoors where signals are often reflected multiple times). Another important point to consider is that even for a constant distance between the devices, the RSSI values can fluctuate very erratically over time. Based on prior work [22] and our own experiments, we can summarize some characteristics of using RSSI for ranging. The following experiments were carried out in a hallway that measures 2.41 m wide × 2.34 m high. The walls are concrete and there are multiple metal doors along them (which help to ensure the presence of multipath). In all cases, a node (either a receiver or transmitter) was affixed to the bottom of an EXIT so that the node was 2.13 m off of the ground while the other node was either carried or set on the ground for each measurement. For BLE experiments, we used Estimote beacons, and, in order to collect the BLE data (RSSI), we developed an application for smart phones using the Estimote SDK. Wi-Fi data were collected using Raspberry Pi 2B (RPi) where the RPis are used for both transmitter and receiver. We wrote some Python code to configure the RPi as a transmitter and set the transmission parameters such as transmission channel, transmission rate, etc. On the receiver side, a Python script was written to scan the channels and record the RSSI. Finally, XBee data were collected through the use of Digi

XBee S2 radio modules with a 2 mW wire antenna and software running on a laptop that uses a remote AT command to get the RSSI of the last received packet. A single RSSI measurement as reported below is actually the median of five such RSSI request values, which provides a rough filtering of outliers. Care was taken to ensure that there were no obstacles between transmitter and receiver for all data collected. That is, there was always a line of sight path between the two nodes.

In stationary cases (i.e., no device mobility and the distance between transmitter and receiver is fixed), RSSI values can fluctuate significantly between adjacent beacons, as shown in **Figures 3–5**. The BLE fluctuation data in **Figure 3** were collected at a distance of 8 m and transmit power of 4 dBm. In **Figure 3**, the RSSI measurements vary by as much as 29 dB over a 45 s period and in **Figure 4**, maximum fluctuations of 10 dB can be observed for XBee radios. The XBee fluctuation data were collected at the same distance and transmit power as the BLE experiment. Finally, **Figure 5** presents the RSSI measurements from Wi-Fi at a distance of 8 m with transmission power of 4 dBm. As can be observed, Wi-Fi shows more stable RSSI behavior with less fluctuation (e.g., less than 10 dBm).

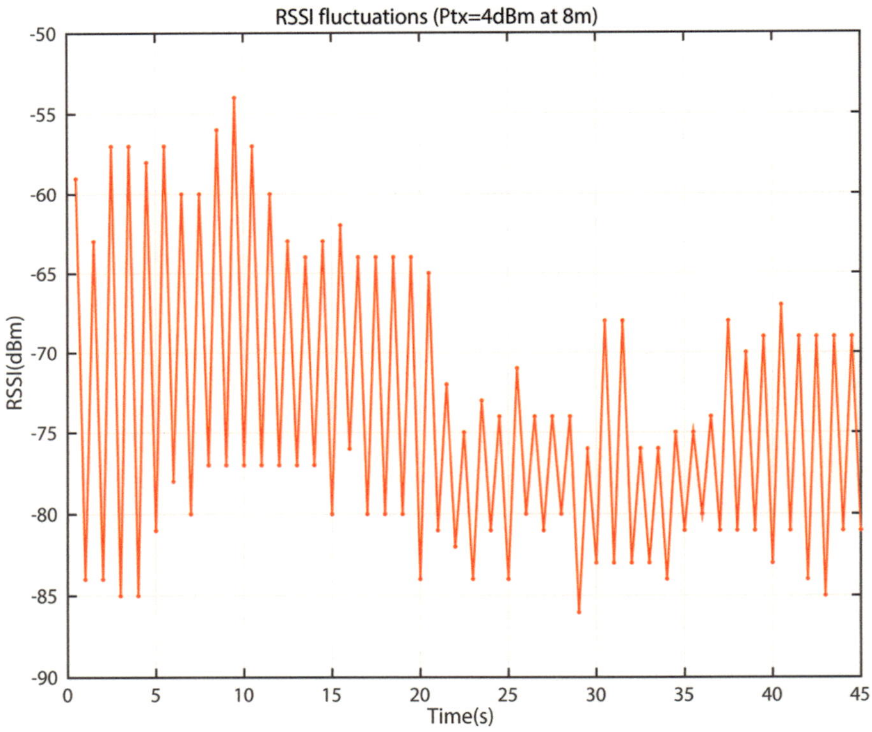

Figure 3. BLE RSSI fluctuations in an indoor environment.

These fluctuations are to be expected because all the walls, doors and floor serve to reflect the signal, which results in many copies of the same packet arriving at the transmitter with varying signal strengths. XBee would appear to be a good choice for communication in the presence of multipath effects due to its lower RSSI fluctuations, but the importance of this metric needs to be balanced with the ability to accurately and reliably relate RSSI to distance. The RSSI value is expected to decrease with increasing distances, but in practice, this relationship is not reliable. As shown in **Figure 6**, the average RSSI does not necessarily decrease as distance increases for BLE, Wi-Fi and XBee (now transmitting at 5 dBm). Note that for BLE, the data were collected while walking away from the EXIT-sign-affixed node at a rate of 0.5 m/s. In particular, for BLE, the average RSSI at a distance of 10 m is greater than the RSSI at a distance of 6 m. A similar behavior can be observed for Wi-Fi signals in **Figure 6**. We note that

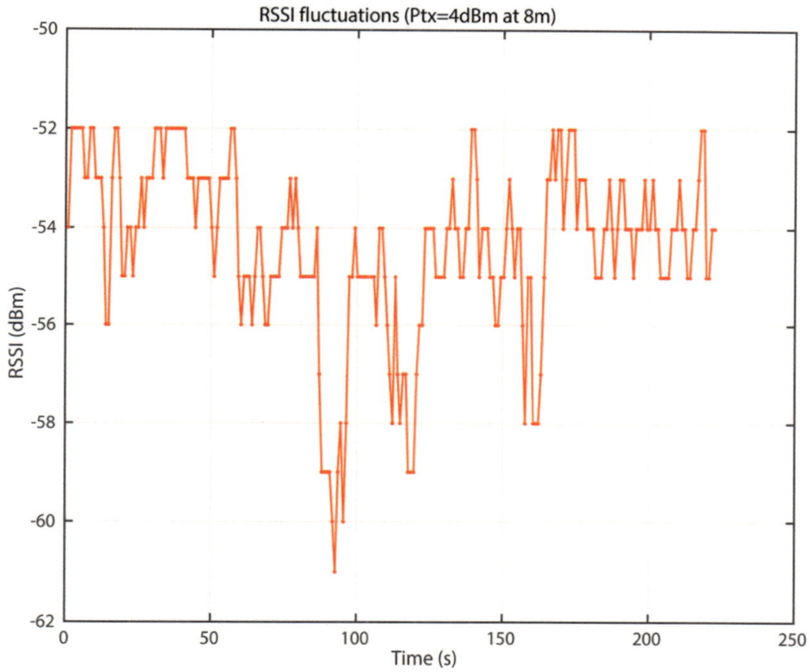

Figure 4. XBee RSSI fluctuations in an indoor environment.

if the RSSI is not averaged then fluctuations such as those illustrated in **Figures 3** and **4** can have a much greater impact on the RSSI-distance trend.

The measured RSSI values typically differ from the expected relationship between signal strength and distance. We performed experiments to show this observation for BLE, Wi-Fi and XBee. In **Figure 7**, we compare the measured RSSI with the mathematical relation between RSSI and distance for BLE presented in Eq. (1) as a function of transmission power, distance (d) and path exponent (n):

$$\text{RSSI} = -(10n\log(d) - A) \tag{1}$$

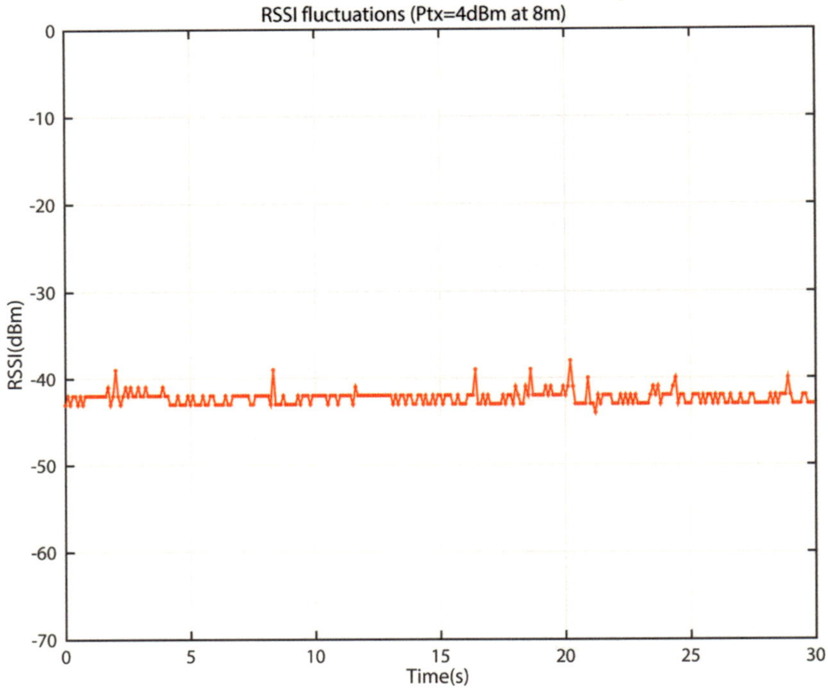

Figure 5. Wi-Fi RSSI fluctuations in an indoor environment.

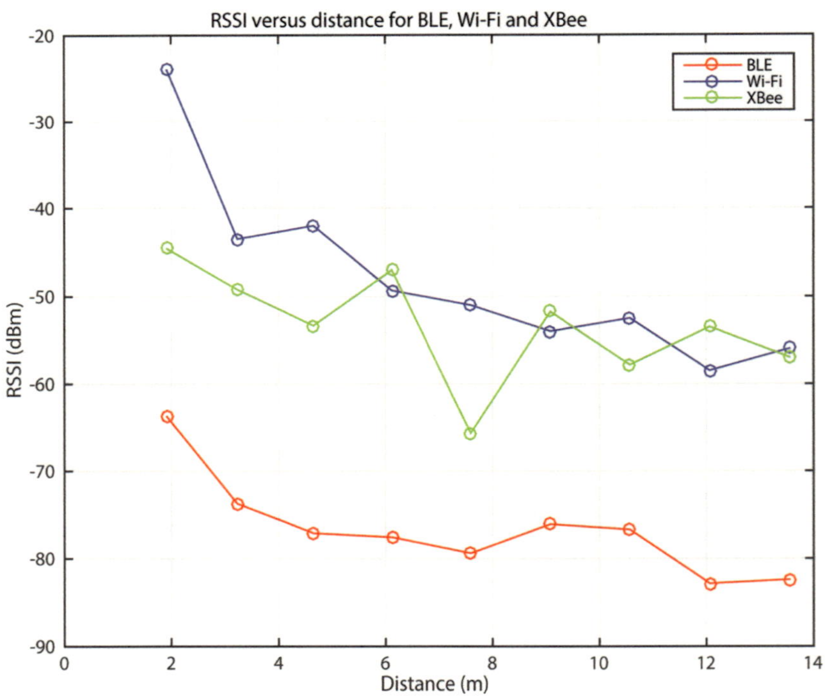

Figure 6. RSSI versus distance for BLE, Wi-Fi and XBee.

http://dx.doi.org/10.5772/66523

In Eq. (1), A is the measured power, which is the expected RSSI value at a distance of 1 m to the BLE beacon. The measured RSSI is a function of transmission power. We performed the same experiment with Wi-Fi to investigate the relation between Wi-Fi RSSI and distance. **Figure 8** shows the comparison of the average of RSSI at different distances with the analytical equation presented in Eq. (2). As can be seen in this equation, the relation between RSSI and distance is a function of frequency f and RSSI.

$$\text{Distance} = 10^{\left(\frac{27.55-(20\log(f))+\text{RSSI}}{20}\right)} \tag{2}$$

Figure 9 shows the relation between RSSI and distance for XBee in the same environment using the same equation as BLE (using different parameters). This figure also indirectly illustrates the sensitivity of radio frequency communication to the environment because here the transmitter was held 1 m off the ground rather than sitting on the ground as shown in **Figure 6** and the relation is much closer to a log relationship between distance and RSSI than the data in **Figure 6**.

The effect of an indoor environment on signal propagation is the primary reason for these data not matching with their respective theoretical model. Any particular packet (or set of packets) may be influenced by multipath despite averaging of results. Additionally, the transmit power, receiver sensitivity and antenna orientation all play a role in influencing RSSI and cause it to no longer follow the theoretical relationship. It is also important to note that the interference from other devices in 2.4 GHz band could have had a hand in driving the measured RSSI away from the expected values.

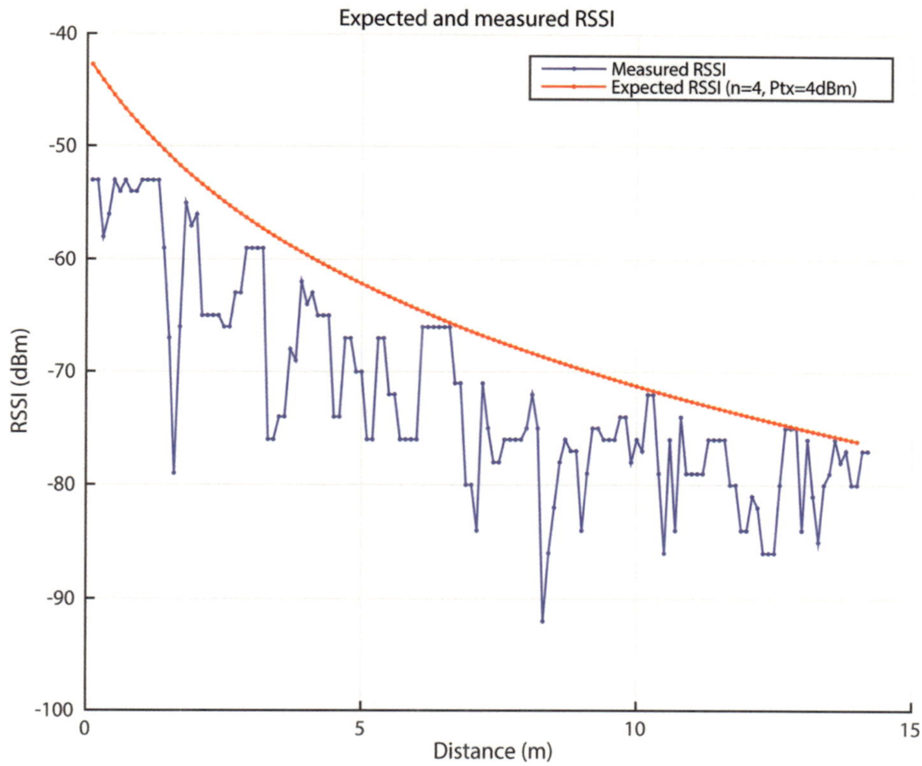

Figure 7. RSSI versus distance for BLE (analytical model and measurements).

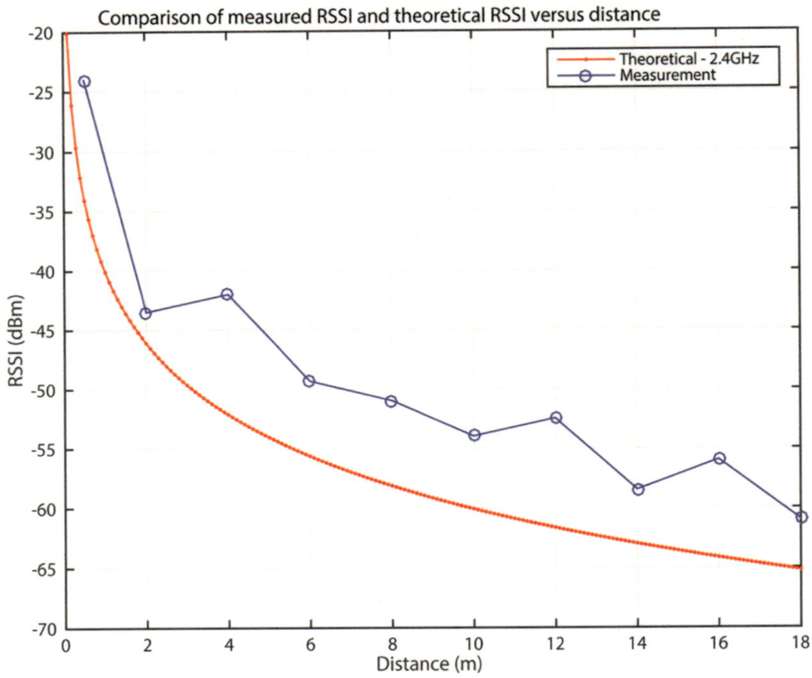

Figure 8. Average RSSI versus distance for Wi-Fi-2.4 GHz (analytical model and measurements).

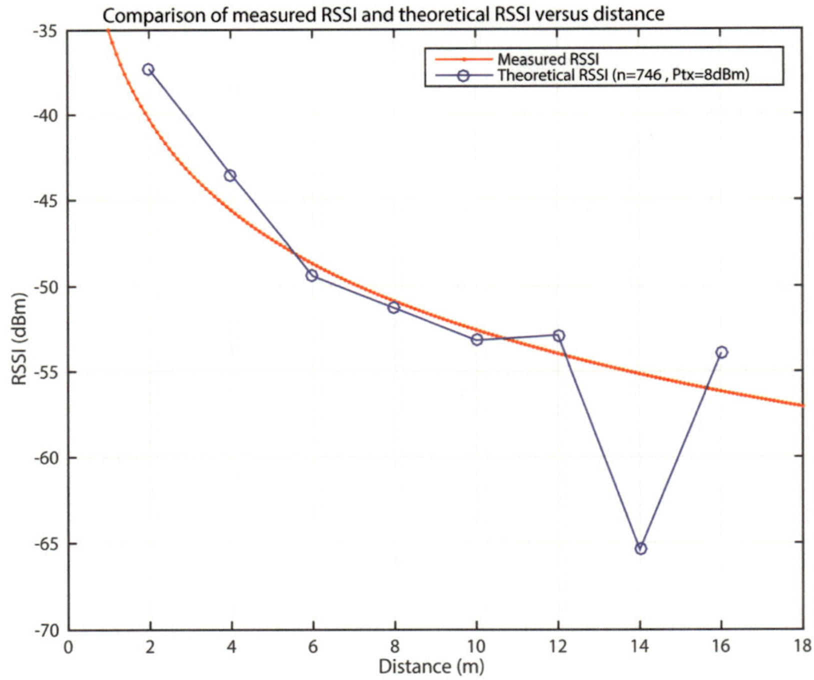

Figure 9. Average RSSI versus distance for XBee radio (analytical model and measurements).

http://dx.doi.org/10.5772/66523

The differences in ranging accuracy are difficult to compare between the different types of radio frequency devices because RSSI is not, by any means, a strictly defined value. Beyond the fact that RSSI is an 8-bit integer representing the strength of the signal, there is little specification as to its implementation. This means that RSSI implementations can differ between vendors of different radio frequency devices and even the same type of radio frequency device.

Finally, as mentioned earlier, the RSSI value fluctuates even for fixed distances between transmitter and receiver. However, these fluctuations vary based on distance, i.e., the larger the distance between transmitter and receiver, the larger the variations observed in the measured RSSI values, as shown in **Table 1**. As shown in **Table 1**, the errors become significantly larger when the receiver is further from a transmitter for BLE beaconing.

Distance (m)	Std. dev. (dBm)	Avg. RSSI (dBm)
3.23	3.76	–63.28
4.65	5.43	–69.60
6.11	4.90	–67.44
7.59	4.64	–65.42
9.07	3.55	–68.57
10.56	6.16	–71.44
12.05	7.89	–74.42
13.55	6.57	–74.28
15.04	7.83	–77.36

Table 1. Average RSSI and standard deviation for BLE.

5. Possible approaches to address the RF-based localization challenges in indoor environments

In the previous section, we reviewed the main challenges of RF-based localization. The main source of these challenges is the structure of indoor environments, which causes multipath effects, heavy shadowing, noise interference and nonline of sight (NLOS) conditions. Additionally, indoor environments must contend with the mobility of obstacles, which has a far greater effect on localization than in an outdoor environment. In the following section, we review various efforts to address these challenges.

5.1. Leveraging channel state information

In recent years, Wi-Fi chipmakers have made channel state information (CSI) per subcarrier (and per antenna) available on their chips. Using a CSI extraction tool, the authors [14, 20, 23] illustrate the use of the channel subcarrier information to achieve decimeter level localization accuracy. In particular, Kotaru et al. [23] use multiple antennas and CSI to calculate the angle of arrival (AoA) and uses a rough estimate of the ToF to provide resilience against multipath effects. Localization is accomplished using a combination of RSSI and AoA for ranging at each anchor. Vasisht et al. [14], as mentioned earlier, use the CSI to calculate the ToF by taking measurements at many different frequencies. Finally, in [20], the authors present Ubicarse, which combines CSI with the gyroscopes in a tablet to realize a synthetic aperture radar (SAR) to carry out localization. The ability to access and analyze this rich source of radio information is incredibly helpful in improving RF-based ranging in an indoor environment and could easily see deployment in an ad-hoc network as long as the hardware and software required to utilize CSI fit within the constraints of the network.

5.2. Calibration

Another technique for improving the reliability of RSSI is using calibration or adding an adjustment factor based on the network parameters such as network dimension, transmission power and number of beacons. The main idea behind the calibration technique is to use the relationship between RSSI and the actual distance between several nodes (usually the anchor nodes with known positions) and utilize it as an offset value to adjust the RSSI for distance estimation. In Ref. [24], the authors attempt to calibrate the RSSI-distance model by using least squares to adjust the reference power at 1 m as well as the path loss exponent. By adaptively calibrating the system, it achieves a lower error and better reliability than methods that only calibrate manually during setup or after a major change. Calibration in this way keeps the range estimation from deteriorating when the environment changes.

As an example of calibration, we implemented a network with three Bluetooth beacons at known locations. We measured the RSSI values at different distances and compare it with the analytical equation as presented in **Figure 7**. To calibrate the ranging measurements, the RSSI was measured between two different pairs of beacons such that the distance separating the pairs was sufficiently dissimilar. Between these new RSSI-distance points, we interpolate a line, which is used to adjust the RSSI measurements. **Figure 10** shows the RSSI-distance graph after using the calibration.

Also, **Figure 11** shows the comparison of the distance error with and without calibration, showing that the calibration can improve the distance estimation error. However, there are still some large peaks in the error graph which illustrate that even with the use of calibration, RSSI is not a completely reliable parameter for distance estimation.

5.3. Adaptive beaconing

Adaptive beaconing is another approach that can be useful for different situations in the network by changing the transmission rate and/or transmission power of the beacons.

Adaptive transmission rate depends on the application of localization. For some applications, such as mobile device tracking and navigation systems, higher transmission rates are needed to keep track of a mobile device. A serious challenge for such systems with high transmission rate is the high packet collision and delay that can affect the localization performance significantly.

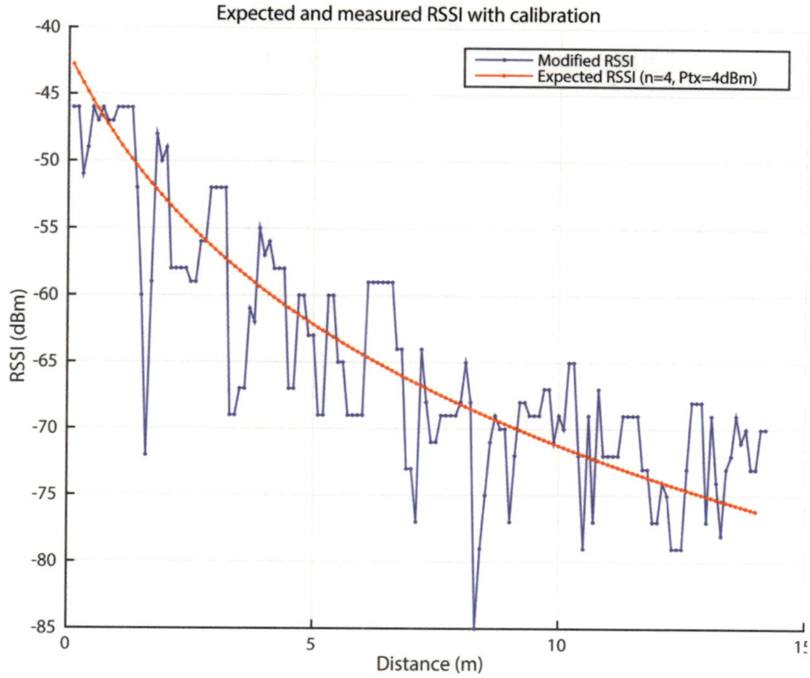

Figure 10. The measured RSSI after calibration.

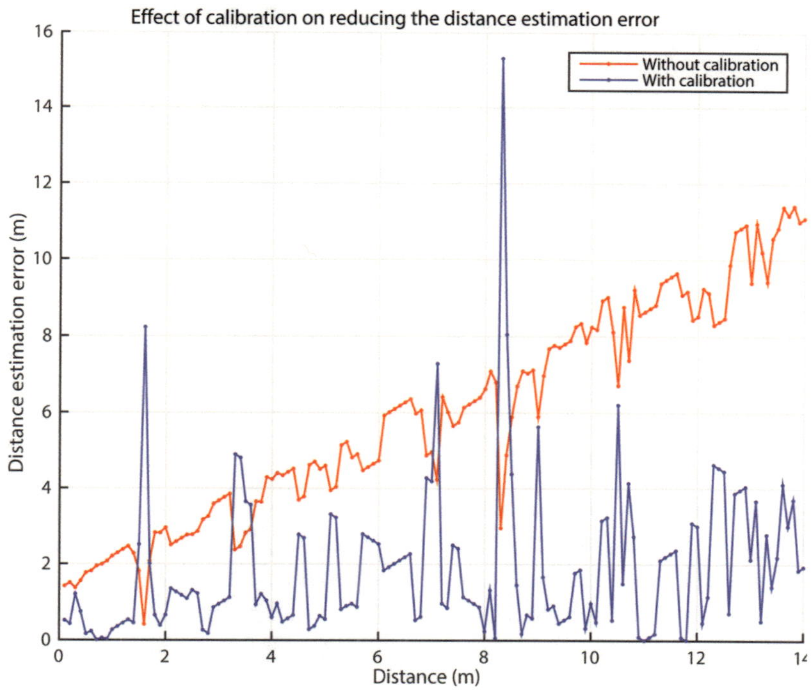

Figure 11. Comparison between distance errors when using the calibration function.

Adaptive transmission power, or multirange beaconing, is an approach that can be utilized to improve the distance estimation for localization purposes. In Ref. [25], the effect of transmission power and number of anchors on accuracy of localization and connectivity of nodes is investigated. In order to evaluate this approach, we ran some experiments by choosing five transmission power levels (–30, –20, –12, –4 and 4 dBm) and measuring the distance error for each transmission power. The average distance error over all transmission powers was also recorded. The measurements were conducted in separate scenarios to avoid any interference. **Figure 12** shows the comparison of the distance error estimation for our measurements. As indicated that with increasing distance, the error increases for each particular transmission power. More importantly, the distance estimation error changes for different transmission powers. Low transmission power can provide very high accuracy distance estimations over short distances from the beacon while high transmission powers are better for distance estimation of greater distances. This illustrates that adapting the transmission power to the distance can provide higher accuracy distance estimation than using a single transmission power alone (or averaging the results of all the transmission powers).

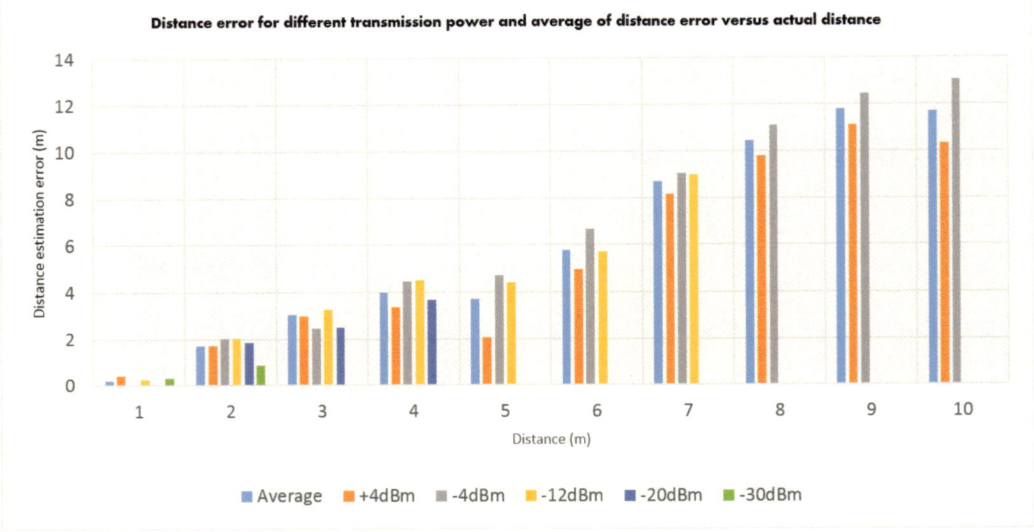

Figure 12. Effect of transmission power on distance estimation error.

5.4. Combination of RF signaling

Another approach for improving the distance estimation and reliability of RSSI is combining different RF-based communication technologies. Recently, Bluetooth-based localization has attracted a lot of attention because of its availability and cost, but many of the efforts rely on unreliable RSSI for proximity extraction in indoor environments. To address this problem, several prior efforts combined Bluetooth beaconing with other technologies such as Wi-Fi [26], Zigbee [27] and RFID [28] to further improve the localization accuracy. Although combining these technologies can improve the localization accuracy, it introduces other challenges such as availability, complexity, or implementation problems that make them less practical solutions.

5.5. Fusing additional sensor data

With the availability of multiple sensors on nodes in some ad-hoc networks, one approach to improve localization estimates is to somehow fuse data from these other sources to, hopefully, cover up some of the shortcomings of RF ranging. For example, ToA and RSSI ranging using anchors can be combined with dead reckoning to improve localization as demonstrated in Refs. [29, 30]. In the former, the authors used two-way time of arrival (TOA) for localization of vehicles in a vehicular network. They assume the existence of a road side unit (RSU) where the vehicles use two-way communication with the RSU and a partial dead reckoning method to determine the position of vehicles in GPS-denied areas. In the latter work, pedestrian dead reckoning location estimates are combined with RSSI localization estimates through the use of an extended Kalman filter (EKF) with some success.

5.6. Cooperative localization

In some network layouts, it is not always possible for every node to communicate with the anchors nodes (if there are any). In such a case, nodes must work together through cooperative localization to figure out where they are all located. Cooperative localization is similar to relative localization but also includes the possibility of some anchors nodes somewhere in the network as well as the potential for fusing additional data from onboard sensors (available in a vehicle or a smartphone) to help localize a node. In [31], pedestrian dead reckoning (PDR) with a smartphone is combined with Wi-Fi RSSI ranging where RSSI is used to determine when two smartphones are near to each other. In this way, the RSSI ranging can help correct heading inaccuracies from PDR. The path that a person takes is abstracted as a series of lines and joints where the RSSI ranging allows for the correction of the joint angles. In Ref. [32], relative localization through ranging is combined with the network topology and graph theory concepts to develop distributed cooperative localization algorithms that can greatly reduced computational complexity and provide resilience to noisy internode measurements. Cooperative localization has great potential in robotics, MANETs and VANETs.

6. Discussion and conclusion

In general, localization in any network can be improved through the exploitation of additional information whether it is from multiple sensors, extra data from the radio, or additional location estimates from neighbors. The goal is to leverage data that is already available so as to not increase the cost or resource requirements of nodes in an ad-hoc network. However, the solutions presented to the above indoor radio frequency localization issues are still not the end of the road for indoor localization or localization in GPS-denied locations. No single solution is going to work everywhere because of constraints on the network, e.g., the availability of particular hardware to carry out localization. Additionally, some networks may not have the luxury of dedicated beacons or anchors, or they may be located in a highly dynamic environment such that RSSI ranging becomes even more troublesome than usual. Finally, on top of the issues of accuracy and cost, there is the issue of the impact of the localization scheme on the performance of the network. The use of passive beacons or active ranging messages could, in the best case, mildly interfere with communication or, at worst, impose a severe restriction on the communication capabilities of the network. The difficulty and importance of indoor localization will ensure that creative and innovative solutions will continue to be sought by those hoping to develop the indoor equivalent of GPS. Whether a single method will satisfy the requirements and constraints of the many disparate networks in use today remains to be seen.

Author details

Mehdi Golestanian, Joshua Siva* and Christian Poellabauer

*Address all correspondence to: joshua.t.siva.1@nd.edu

University of Notre Dame, Notre Dame, Indiana, USA

References

[1] Dargie W, Poellabauer C. Fundamentals of wireless sensor networks: theory and practice. West Sussex: John Wiley & Sons; 2010 Nov 5.

[2] Kim DY, Kim SH, Choi D, Jin SH. Accurate Indoor Proximity Zone Detection Based on Time Window and Frequency with Bluetooth Low Energy. Procedia Computer Science. 2015 Dec 31;56:88–95.

[3] Ahmed I, Orfali S, Khattab T, Mohamed A. Characterization of the indoor-outdoor radio propagation channel at 2.4 GHz. In GCC Conference and Exhibition (GCC) 2011 Feb 19 (pp. 605–608). IEEE.

[4] Chen Y, Lymberopoulos D, Liu J, Priyantha B. FM-based indoor localization. In Proceedings of the 10th international conference on Mobile systems, applications and services 2012 Jun 25 (pp. 169–182). ACM.

[5] Chintalapudi K, Padmanabha Iyer A, Padmanabhan VN. Indoor localization without the pain. In Proceedings of the sixteenth annual international conference on Mobile computing and networking 2010 Sep 20 (pp. 173–184). ACM.

[6] Hossain AM, Soh WS. A comprehensive study of bluetooth signal parameters for localization. In 2007 IEEE 18th International Symposium on Personal, Indoor and Mobile Radio Communications. 2007 Sep 3 (pp. 1–5). IEEE.

[7] Kim DY, Kim SH, Choi D, Jin SH. Accurate Indoor Proximity Zone Detection Based on Time Window and Frequency with Bluetooth Low Energy. Procedia Computer Science. 2015 Dec 31;56:88–95.

[8] Al Nuaimi K, Kamel H. A survey of indoor positioning systems and algorithms. In Innovations in information technology (IIT), 2011 international conference on 2011 Apr 25 (pp. 185–190). IEEE.

[9] Hossain AM, Soh WS. A survey of calibration-free indoor positioning systems. Computer Communications. 2015 Jul 15;66:1–3.

[10] Ravi N, Shankar P, Frankel A, Elgammal A, Iftode L. Indoor localization using camera phones. InSeventh IEEE Workshop on Mobile Computing Systems & Applications (WMCSA'06 Supplement) 2006 Apr 6 (pp. 49–49). IEEE.

[11] Chen W, Mei T, Sun L, Liu Y, Li Y, Li S, Liang H, Meng MQ. Error analyzing for RSSI-based localization in wireless sensor networks. In Intelligent Control and Automation. WCICA 2008. 7th World Congress on 2008 Jun 25 (pp. 2701–2706). IEEE.

[12] Cheon J, Hwang H, Kim D, Jung Y. IEEE 802.15. 4 ZigBee-Based Time-of-Arrival Estimation for Wireless Sensor Networks. Sensors. 2016 Feb 5;16(2):203.

[13] Silva B, Pang Z, Åkerberg J, Neander J, Hancke G. Experimental study of UWB-based high precision localization for industrial applications. In 2014 IEEE International Conference on Ultra-WideBand (ICUWB) 2014 Sep 1 (pp. 280–285). IEEE.

[14] Vasisht D, Kumar S, Katabi D. Decimeter-level localization with a single WiFi access point. In 13th USENIX Symposium on Networked Systems Design and Implementation (NSDI 16) 2016 (pp. 165–178).

[15] Chen J, Wu XJ, Wen PZ, Ye F, Liu JW. A new distributed localization algorithm for ZigBee wireless networks. In Control and Decision Conference, 2009. CCDC'09. Chinese 2009 Jun 17 (pp. 4451–4456). IEEE.

[16] Jiang JA, Zheng XY, Chen YF, Wang CH, Chen PT, Chuang CL, Chen CP. A distributed RSS-based localization using a dynamic circle expanding mechanism. IEEE Sensors Journal. 2013 Oct;13(10):3754–3766.

[17] Sugano M, Kawazoe T, Ohta Y, Murata M. Indoor localization system using RSSI measurement of wireless sensor network based on ZigBee standard. Target. 2006 Jul;538:050.

[18] El Madani B, Yao AP, Lyhyaoui A. Combining Kalman filtering with ZigBee protocol to improve localization in wireless sensor network. ISRN Sensor Networks [Internet]. 2013 Mar 21 [cited 2016 Jul 25]; 2013(252056):1–7. Available from: https://www.hindawi.com/journals/isrn/2013/252056/ DOI: 10.1155/2013/252056.

[19] Kwak M, Chong J. A new double two-way ranging algorithm for ranging system. In Network Infrastructure and Digital Content, 2010 2nd IEEE International Conference on 2010 Sep 24 (pp. 470–473). IEEE.

[20] Kumar S, Gil S, Katabi D, Rus D. Accurate indoor localization with zero start-up cost. In Proceedings of the 20th annual international conference on Mobile computing and networking 2014 Sep 7 (pp. 483–494). ACM.

[21] Niculescu D, Nath B. DV based positioning in ad hoc networks. Telecommunication Systems. 2003 Jan 1;22(1–4):267–280.

[22] Golestanian M, Poellabauer C. Indoor localization using multi-range beaconing: poster. In Proceedings of the 17th ACM International Symposium on Mobile Ad Hoc Networking and Computing 2016 Jul 5 (pp. 397–398). ACM.

[23] Kotaru M, Joshi K, Bharadia D, Katti S. Spotfi: Decimeter level localization using wifi. In Proceedings of the 2015 ACM Conference on Special Interest Group on Data Communication 2015 Aug 17 (pp. 269–282). ACM.

[24] Bernardos AM, Casar JR, Tarrío P. Real time calibration for rss indoor positioning systems. In Indoor Positioning and Indoor Navigation (IPIN), 2010 International Conference on 2010 Sep 15 (pp. 1–7). IEEE.

[25] Vivekanandan V, Wong VW. Concentric anchor beacon localization algorithm for wireless sensor networks. IEEE transactions on vehicular technology. 2007 Sep;56(5):2733–2744.

[26] Galván-Tejada C.E., Carrasco-Jiménez J.C. Brena, R.F. Bluetooth-WiFi based combined positioning algorithm, implementation and experimental evaluation. Procedia Technology. 2013; 7: 37–45.

[27] Dahlgren E, Mahmood H. Evaluation of indoor positioning based on Bluetooth Smart technology. Master of Science Thesis in the Programme Computer Systems and Networks. 2014.

[28] Liu J. Survey of Wireless Based Indoor Localization Technologies. Department of Science & Engineering, Washington University. 2014.

[29] Wahab A.A, Khattab A, Fahmy Y.A. Two-way TOA with limited dead reckoning for GPS-free vehicle localization using single RSU. In ITS Telecommunications (ITST), 2013 13th International Conference on 2013 Nov. (pp. 244–249). IEEE.

[30] Zhuang Y, El-Sheimy N. Tightly-Coupled Integration of WiFi and MEMS Sensors on Handheld Devices for Indoor Pedestrian Navigation. Sensors Journal, IEEE. 2016 Jan 1;16(1):224–34.

[31] Iwase T, Shibasaki R. Infra-free indoor positioning using only smartphone sensors. In Indoor Positioning and Indoor Navigation (IPIN), 2013 International Conference on 2013 Oct 28 (pp. 1–8). IEEE.

[32] Eren T. Cooperative localization in wireless ad hoc and sensor networks using hybrid distance and bearing (angle of arrival) measurements. EURASIP Journal on Wireless Communications and Networking. 2011 Dec 1;2011(1):1–8.